CONTENTS

INTRODUCTION
2

APPETIZERS
6

BRUNCH
28

MAIN DISHES
48

DESSERTS
74

INDEX
96

A note on nutrition: All recipes in this cookbook were developed and tested in The Pampered Chef Test Kitchens by professional home economists. Nutritional content of these recipes is based on food composition data in The Pampered Chef data base. Variations in ingredients, products and measurements may result in approximate values. Each analysis is based on ingredients initially listed and does not include optional ingredients, garnishes, fat used to grease pans or serving suggestions, unless noted. Recipes requiring ground turkey are analyzed based on 97 percent lean ground turkey. Recipes requiring ground beef are based on 90 percent lean ground beef.

CLOCKWISE FROM BOTTOM LEFT: 13" ROUND BAKING STONE W/OVEN-TO-TABLE RACK, 9" PIE PLATE, 9" x 13" BAKER, MINI-BAKING BOWL, 15" ROUND BAKING STONE, DEEP DISH BAKER, BAKING BOWL, LOAF PAN AND 12" x 15" RECTANGLE BAKING STONE. CENTER: 8" MINI-BAKER, 9" SQUARE BAKER.

THE PAMPERED CHEF'S FAMILY HERITAGE™ STONEWARE COLLECTION

SENSATIONAL STONEWARE

A Cook's Best Friend

Consider yourself one smart cook. Why? You are the proud owner of one or more pieces in The Pampered Chef's Family Heritage™ Stoneware Collection. It means you have an eye for quality, value and high performance. Whether you are just beginning to collect this fine stoneware or you already have a number of pieces, you can make the most of your wise investment by using your *Stoneware Sensations* cookbook. Let it inspire the creative cook in you!

Getting to Know Your Stoneware

Before you turn your culinary inspirations loose in the kitchen, take a few moments to read the following information. In addition to a few fun, informative facts about the history and makeup of stoneware, you will learn how to use, care for and maximize the benefits of your Family Heritage™ Collection. Even if you are an experienced stoneware baker, these hints and guidelines will enhance your baking success.

From Stone-Age Clay to Stoneware

Did you know that every time you use your Family Heritage™ Stoneware you are practicing an ancient cooking method? Our early ancestors discovered that heating a clay vessel in fire hardened it, thereby making it more durable. While it was an improvement over nonfired clay vessels, this early pottery was very porous and had a short life expectancy. The ancient Chinese are credited with inventing stoneware as we know it today. Chinese potters were able to build kilns that could reach at least 2000°F — the temperature needed to transform clay into a stone-hard, virtually nonporous substance.

Today, The Pampered Chef continues to use this same age-old technique that transforms clay into durable, naturally beautiful stoneware. The fact that we are still using stoneware centuries later is a testimonial to this outstanding cooking method.

Red Clay Bakeware vs. Stoneware

There are two basic types of clay bakeware available today: red clay and stoneware. What is the difference? The clay used in red clay bakeware has a low melting point and cannot withstand the high kiln temperatures needed to produce stoneware. Therefore, unglazed red clay bakeware is porous, more fragile than stoneware and must be soaked in water before it goes into the oven. Although glazed red clay does not require soaking, the glaze reduces the desirable brick-oven effect of clay cookery.

In contrast, Family Heritage™ Stoneware is made from natural grey stoneware clay. When fired at over 2000°F temperatures, this clay produces an unglazed, buff-colored stoneware that is unaffected by moisture and completely safe for use with food. As a result, no glazing or soaking is required. After firing, each Family Heritage™ piece is hand finished, producing a one-of-a-kind creation. This is why no two pieces of stoneware look or feel exactly alike. The benefits of baking with Family Heritage™ Stoneware are numerous. Because it heats evenly and then retains that heat, it produces exceptionally crisp crusts and moist interiors, promotes even baking and browning, and roasts foods to perfection. In short, it gives you all the incredible baking advantages of an authentic brick-lined oven!

Caring for Your Stoneware

Using and caring for your Family Heritage™ Stoneware is as easy as any other type of high-quality bakeware. Practicing a few simple steps will keep your stoneware in great shape and performing well year after year. While most of this information can be found in the instructions accompanying your stoneware, read through it again here to make sure you are following these important guidelines.

Preparing Your Stoneware for Use

Before using your stoneware for the first time, follow these simple steps. Remember, do *not* soak stoneware in water before using.

- Rinse the stoneware in warm water, then towel dry.
- Season the stoneware by baking a high-fat food, such as refrigerated crescent rolls or cookie dough, on its surface. Afterwards, greasing is usually unnecessary. If food does stick slightly, you may *lightly* spray the surface with vegetable oil spray for the next few uses.

General Guidelines for Use

The most important fact to remember about your stoneware is that it doesn't like extreme and sudden temperature changes or what is called thermal shock. Despite its durability, ceramic is not indestructible. If you expose your stoneware to sudden temperature changes, it may develop small hairline cracks or break. By practicing the following guidelines, your stoneware will last for many years.

- Always use a stoneware piece that closely matches the size of the food item being prepared.
- Thick, dense frozen foods, such as chicken parts, fish fillets or pork chops, should be thawed completely before cooking. Putting a frozen pizza or frozen precooked foods, such as chicken nuggets, French fries and fish sticks, on stoneware is fine. Just be sure to evenly distribute small pieces over the surface.
- Allow hot stoneware to cool completely before immersing it in water or pouring water or other liquids into or onto it.
- Stoneware cannot be used under the broiler or directly over a heat source, such as a range-top burner.
- Always preheat the oven before baking foods in stoneware. However, do *not* preheat empty stoneware in the oven because this may cause the stoneware to crack or break.
- Stoneware is freezer safe. However, do not transfer any stoneware piece directly from the freezer to the oven. Allow foods frozen in the stoneware to thaw completely in the refrigerator before placing them in the oven to bake.
- Use the same baking times and temperatures with stoneware as you would with other bakeware. The only exception is if the food requires a baking time under 10 minutes. You may need to bake these items an additional 1 to 2 minutes. When baking cookies, for example, the first batch may need a few extra minutes, but the following batches will bake in the specified amount of time.
- Stoneware is microwave safe. However, foods will not become crisp or brown in the microwave oven.
- When using stoneware in a convection oven, remember to reduce the oven temperature and baking time by the amount specified in the oven's use and care manual. If foods are browning too quickly, lightly cover the surface of the food with aluminum foil for part of the baking time.

- Always use a heavy, heat-resistant potholder or oven pad when handling hot stoneware. It becomes extremely hot both in the oven and microwave oven.
- Foods may be cut directly on the stoneware for serving.

Seasoning Your Stoneware to Perfection

When you prepare your stoneware for the first time, you begin the natural seasoning process. Seasoning occurs when fats and oils from foods gradually adhere to the stoneware's surface. It is perfectly natural for this to occur and does not pose a threat to food safety. As your stoneware becomes increasingly seasoned, it forms a nonstick coating. The color of your stoneware will also gradually change from its natural buff color to a deep brown. If you prefer to have your bakeware look brand new, you will need to get used to the idea that stoneware performs best when it looks like it's been used. In fact, the darker its surface becomes, the better its baking qualities. If you have a well-seasoned steel wok or cast-iron skillet, the concept is the same.

Cleaning Your Stoneware is Easy

Believe it or not, cleaning your stoneware is the easiest part of its care. Because you want to keep the seasoning on the surface intact, only gentle cleaning is required. In fact, it is important that you do not use soap or detergent when cleaning stoneware. The soap will attach itself to the fats and oils in the seasoning and remain on the surface, giving a soapy flavor to the next foods that are baked on it. For the same reason, stoneware should not be washed in a dishwasher. Here are the simple steps for cleaning:

- Allow the stoneware to cool completely before cleaning.

- Scrape off any excess food using the nylon pan scraper that came with your stoneware or simply use a nylon spatula.
- If necessary, soak the stoneware in clear, hot water to loosen baked-on foods.
- Rinse and dry thoroughly.

If you follow these simple cleaning instructions, the stoneware cannot harbor any harmful bacteria that would pose a threat to food safety. The surface of the stoneware is clean and safe to use as long as all food particles have been removed and the stoneware is dried thoroughly before storing.

Handling and Storing Your Stoneware

A little tender loving care will prevent your stoneware from cracking or breaking. Avoid dropping stoneware or knocking it against a hard surface. Don't stack stoneware pieces or place other heavy utensils, such as bowls or cookware, on top of them. If you must store your stoneware on a rack in the oven, be sure to remove all the pieces before turning on the oven.

It's Time to Start Baking

Now that you are an expert on stoneware, it's time to start baking! You, your family and guests will savor this delectable assortment of appetizers, main dishes, brunch dishes and desserts. Suitable for quick everyday meals, potluck suppers and entertaining, these recipes are sure to become your new all-time favorites. And you will be delighted by the superb baking results of your Family Heritage™ Stoneware. So roll up your sleeves, turn on your oven and get ready for all the compliments you are about to receive!

GARDEN SEAFOOD PIZZA P. 8

APPETIZERS

We've assembled a number
of the latest party pleasers
and some that are destined
to become all-time favorites.
Most are extremely simple
to prepare and made especially
good with our flat Baking
Stones and Bakers. Breads,
tortillas and pizza crusts will
be crisper, meats will be juicier,
and you will discover your
Stoneware to be your best
friend in the kitchen.

GARDEN SEAFOOD PIZZA

Refrigerated crescent rolls make a perfectly simple pizza crust. This appetizer pizza features a topping of herbed cream cheese, fresh chopped spinach, and a hint of lemon. Chopped crabmeat and ripe olives add the finishing touches.

1 package (8 ounces) refrigerated crescent rolls

1½ cups firmly packed fresh spinach leaves, stemmed and coarsely chopped

1 package (8 ounces) cream cheese, softened

1 green onion with top, sliced

½ teaspoon dill weed

⅛ teaspoon ground black pepper

1 teaspoon lemon zest, divided

½ teaspoon lemon juice

4 ounces flake- or leg-style imitation crabmeat, coarsely chopped

¼ cup pitted ripe olives, coarsely chopped

Preheat oven to 350°F. Unroll crescent dough; separate into triangles. On **13" Round Baking Stone**, arrange triangles in circle with points in the center and wide ends toward the outside. Using lightly floured **Dough and Pizza Roller**, roll out dough to 12-inch circle, pressing seams together to seal. Bake 12-15 minutes or until golden brown. Remove from oven. Cool completely. Using **Food Chopper**, chop spinach in 3 batches. In **1-Qt. Batter Bowl**, combine cream cheese, 1 cup of the spinach, green onion, dill weed, pepper, ½ teaspoon of the lemon zest and lemon juice; mix well. Spread cream cheese mixture evenly onto crust. Using Food Chopper, coarsely chop crabmeat and olives. Top pizza with remaining spinach, crabmeat, olives and remaining ½ teaspoon lemon zest. Cut pizza using **Pizza Cutter**; serve with **Mini-Serving Spatula.**

Yield: 10 servings

Approximately 180 calories and 14 grams of fat per serving

COOK'S TIPS

■ *Tightly pack the spinach leaves under the* **Food Chopper** *for easier chopping.*

■ *For extra convenience, buy prepackaged, washed fresh spinach. Any leftover spinach can be used in your favorite salad.*

■ *Reduced-fat cream cheese may be substituted for the regular cream cheese.*

HAWAIIAN MEATBALLS

Flavored with pineapple and ginger, these saucy meatballs bring you the taste of the islands. Serve on party picks with juicy pineapple chunks. Aloha!

2 cans (8 ounces each) pineapple chunks
   in juice, undrained
½ cup red or green bell pepper, chopped
1 teaspoon fresh ginger root, chopped
1 pound ground fresh turkey
½ cup green onion slices
½ cup plain dry bread crumbs
½ teaspoon salt
1 cup teriyaki sauce

Preheat oven to 400°F. Drain pineapple, reserving juice; set aside. Using **Food Chopper**, finely chop bell pepper and ginger root. In **Classic 2-Qt. Batter Bowl**, combine ¼ cup of the pineapple juice, bell pepper, ginger root, turkey, green onion, bread crumbs and salt; mix gently but thoroughly. Using small **Stainless Steel Scoop**, shape meat mixture into balls; place in **Deep Dish Baker**. Pour teriyaki sauce over meatballs; mix lightly to coat meatballs evenly. Bake 30 minutes. Place 1 piece of pineapple on each party pick. Add meatball and serve.

Yield: 40 meatballs

Approximately 80 calories and 3 grams of fat per serving (2 meatballs)

COOK'S TIP

■ *Store ginger root in a resealable plastic bag in the refrigerator for up to 3 weeks or in the freezer for up to 6 months. If using frozen ginger root, just slice off as much as you need before returning the unused portion to the freezer.*

TOOL TIP

■ *Ginger root has a smooth, tan-colored skin that should be removed before use. Use our **3" Self-Sharpening Paring Knife** to carefully remove the paper-thin skin from the delicate, flavorful flesh. Chop or, for minced ginger root, place a small chunk of it in the **Garlic Press** and squeeze.*

TOMATO-BASIL SQUARES

*Nothing quite compares to the sweet taste of ripe tomatoes and
fresh basil atop creamy mozzarella and fresh Parmesan cheeses.
It's a simple appetizer that gets rave reviews.*

1 package (10 ounces) refrigerated pizza
  crust
2 cups (8 ounces) shredded
  mozzarella cheese, divided
1 ounce (¼ cup) fresh Parmesan cheese,
  grated
2 tablespoons fresh basil leaves, snipped, or
  2 teaspoons dried basil leaves
⅔ cup mayonnaise
1 garlic clove, pressed
4 plum tomatoes, thinly sliced

Preheat oven to 375°F. Using lightly floured **Dough
and Pizza Roller**, roll out pizza crust on **12" x 15"
Rectangle Baking Stone** to within 1 inch of edge of
Stone. Sprinkle crust with 1 cup of the mozzarella
cheese; set aside. Using **Deluxe Cheese Grater**, grate
Parmesan cheese. Using **Kitchen Cutters**, snip basil.
In **1-Qt. Batter Bowl**, combine the remaining 1 cup
mozzarella cheese, Parmesan cheese, basil and
mayonnaise; mix well. Using **Garlic Press**, press garlic
over cheese mixture; mix well. Using **Vario-Slicer**,
thinly slice tomatoes; arrange in single layer over
mozzarella cheese on crust. Using medium **Stainless
Steel Scoop**, place mozzarella cheese mixture over
tomatoes; spread to cover evenly. Bake 15-20
minutes or until top is golden brown and bubbly.
Serve warm. Cut with **Pizza Cutter**; serve with
Mini-Serving Spatula.

Yield: 20 servings

Approximately 130 calories and 9 grams of fat per serving

COOK'S TIP

■ *Gently wash fresh basil leaves just before
using and blot dry with a paper towel. Wrap in
a damp paper towel, place in a resealable
plastic bag, and refrigerate for up to 1 week.
Use as a garnish or as a flavor booster for
soups, sauces, salads or salad dressing.*

TOOL TIP

■ *For a quick way to snip fresh herbs without the
mess, place herb in small bowl; snip with
Kitchen Cutters.*

TOMATO-BASIL SQUARES

TANGY FRUIT SALSA WITH CINNAMON CHIPS

Sweeten your options with this raspberry, peach and kiwifruit salsa.
Cinnamon tortilla chips, baked to perfection on
our flat Baking Stone, are the ultimate dippers.

Cinnamon Chips

1	tablespoon sugar
¼	teaspoon ground cinnamon
4	(7-inch) flour tortillas

Salsa

1	cup frozen raspberries
2	peaches, peeled and chopped
2	kiwifruit, peeled, sliced and quartered
1	teaspoon lime zest
2	teaspoons lime juice
1	teaspoon sugar

For cinnamon chips, preheat oven to 400°F. In **Flour/Sugar Shaker**, combine sugar and cinnamon. Using **Kitchen Spritzer**, lightly spray tortillas with water; sprinkle with cinnamon-sugar mixture. Using **Pizza Cutter**, cut each tortilla into 8 wedges; place in single layer on flat **Baking Stone**. Bake 8-10 minutes or until lightly browned and crisp. Remove to **Nonstick Cooling Rack**; cool completely.

Meanwhile for salsa, place raspberries in **1-Qt. Batter Bowl**. Using **Food Chopper**, chop peaches. Slice kiwifruit with **Egg Slicer Plus**; cut into quarters. Combine all salsa ingredients in Batter Bowl; mix gently. Serve with cinnamon chips.

Yield: 2 cups salsa and 32 chips (16 servings)

Approximately 80 calories and 1 gram of fat per serving (2 tablespoons salsa and 2 chips)

COOK'S TIP

■ *One can (15 or 16 ounces) peaches in juice, drained and chopped, may be substituted for the fresh peaches, if desired.*

CHICKEN SATAY WITH PEANUT DIPPING SAUCE

Transform ordinary chicken into an extraordinary hors d'oeuvre with this tangy, sweet marinade of lime juice, brown sugar, soy sauce and garlic.

⅓ cup soy sauce
⅓ cup packed brown sugar
2 teaspoons lime zest
¼ cup lime juice
3 garlic cloves, pressed
1½ pounds boneless, skinless chicken breasts, cut into 1-inch pieces
⅓ cup creamy peanut butter
1 tablespoon snipped fresh cilantro

In **Classic 2-Qt. Batter Bowl**, combine soy sauce, brown sugar, lime zest and juice. Using **Garlic Press**, press garlic into soy sauce mixture; mix well. Reserve ⅓ cup soy sauce mixture for Peanut Dipping Sauce; place in **1-Qt. Batter Bowl**. Set aside. Add chicken to remaining soy sauce mixture in 2-Qt. Batter Bowl. Cover; marinate in refrigerator 30 minutes.

Preheat oven to 400°F. Place chicken with marinade in **9" Square Baker**. Bake 18-20 minutes or until chicken is no longer pink in center. Meanwhile, prepare Peanut Dipping Sauce by adding peanut butter and cilantro to reserved ⅓ cup soy sauce mixture in 1-Qt. Batter Bowl; whisk until smooth with **10" Whisk**. Serve with chicken.

Yield: 12 servings

Approximately 130 calories and 4 grams of fat per serving
(4 chicken pieces and 1 tablespoon sauce)

COOK'S TIPS

■ *Also known as coriander or Chinese parsley, cilantro is a fresh herb with bright green leaves resembling flat-leaf parsley.*

■ *To store cilantro, place, stem ends down, in a glass filled with enough water to cover 1 inch of the stems. Cover loosely with a plastic bag and refrigerate for up to 5 days.*

FIESTA NACHOS

*Treat your guests to authentic, crispy, homemade nacho chips baked on
our 15" Round Baking Stone. Top with your favorite south-of-the-border ingredients
and heat until cheese is melted. ¡Olé!*

6 (7-inch) flour tortillas
1 can (15 ounces) black beans, rinsed and drained
4 green onions with tops, thinly sliced
3 tablespoons salsa
2 cups (8 ounces) shredded Mexican-style cheese, divided
½ cup tomato, chopped
 Sour cream (optional)
 Guacamole (optional)

Preheat oven to 400°F. Using **Pizza Cutter**, cut each tortilla into 6 wedges. Starting at outside edge of **15" Round Baking Stone**, arrange tortilla wedges in circle with sides slightly overlapping and points toward center. Repeat with remaining tortilla wedges to form additional overlapping rows of chips. (Entire surface of Stone will be covered with chips.) Bake 8-10 minutes or until chips are lightly browned and crisp; remove from oven. In **1-Qt. Batter Bowl**, combine beans, green onions and salsa; mix gently. Sprinkle 1 cup of the cheese evenly over tortilla chips on Stone; top with bean mixture and the remaining 1 cup cheese. Bake 3 minutes or just until cheese is melted; remove from oven. Chop tomato with **Food Chopper**; sprinkle over nachos. Serve warm with sour cream, guacamole and additional salsa, if desired.

Yield: 12 servings

Approximately 150 calories and 8 grams of fat per serving

COOK'S TIPS

- *Mexican-style cheese is a combination of pre-packaged shredded natural cheeses including cheddar, colby and Monterey Jack.*

- *In a crunch for time? Try prepared guacamole, which is available in the refrigerated or frozen food section of most supermarkets.*

TOOL TIP

- *For ease of preparation, stack 2 tortillas before cutting into wedges with **Pizza Cutter**.*

WESTERN POTATO ROUNDS

Use the Garnisher to crinkle cut the potatoes into attractive slices.
Bake them on our 15" Round Baking Stone, then brush with
barbecue sauce before topping with the flavorful toppers.

2   large unpeeled baking potatoes
      (about 1¼ pounds)
      Vegetable oil
1   cup (4 ounces) shredded Co-Jack cheese
6   bacon slices, crisply cooked, drained and
      crumbled
⅓   cup green onion slices
¼   cup barbecue sauce

Preheat oven to 450°F. Using **Garnisher**, cut potatoes into ¼-inch-thick slices. Using **Kitchen Spritzer**, generously spray both sides of potato slices with oil; place on **15" Round Baking Stone**. Bake 20 minutes or until lightly browned; remove from oven. In **1-Qt. Batter Bowl**, combine cheese, bacon and green onion. Using **Pastry Brush**, generously brush potato slices with barbecue sauce; sprinkle with cheese mixture. Return potato slices to oven. Bake 3-5 minutes or until cheese is melted.

Yield: 24 rounds

Approximately 120 calories and 7 grams of fat per serving
(2 potato rounds)

COOK'S TIPS

- *Leaving the peel on the potatoes will help keep the shape of the baked potato slices.*

- *The potato slices will cook more evenly when sliced to the same thickness.*

TOOL TIP

- *Use the **Garnisher** to create an attractive scalloped edge on vegetables, hard-cooked eggs and cheese.*

WESTERN POTATO ROUNDS

MINI SOFT PRETZELS WITH HONEY-MUSTARD DIP

Our Baking Stone transforms purchased refrigerated pizza dough into delicious, soft pretzels.

Mini Pretzels
- 1 package (10 ounces) refrigerated pizza crust
- 1 egg, lightly beaten
- ½ teaspoon salt
- 1 tablespoon caraway seeds or sesame seeds

Honey-Mustard Dip
- ¾ cup mayonnaise
- 3 tablespoons Dijon mustard
- 3 tablespoons honey

Preheat oven to 425°F. For mini pretzels, unroll pizza crust onto flat side of **18" x 12" Grooved Cutting Board**. Using **Pizza Cutter**, cut dough lengthwise into eighteen ½-inch-wide strips. Form each strip into pretzel shape. Place on **15" Round Baking Stone**. In small bowl, combine egg and salt; brush onto dough using **Pastry Brush**. Sprinkle with seeds. Bake 10-12 minutes or until golden brown. Remove immediately to **Nonstick Cooling Rack**. For honey-mustard dip, whisk together all dip ingredients in **1-Qt. Batter Bowl** with **10" Whisk** until well blended. Serve with warm pretzels.

Yield: 18 mini pretzels and 1 cup dip

Approximately 130 calories and 9 grams of fat per serving (1 pretzel and 1 tablespoon dip)

Pretzel Stick Twists: Unroll pizza dough and cut into nine 1-inch-wide lengthwise strips. Cut each strip crosswise in half. For each pretzel stick, hold both ends of 1 dough strip and twist in opposite directions; place on 15" Round Baking Stone to secure twist. Proceed as recipe directs.

COOK'S TIPS

- *The egg glaze adds color and shine to the baked pretzels, while also serving to hold the seeds in place.*

- *Coarse salt may be substituted for the seeds, if desired.*

REUBEN ROLL-UPS

Named after the famous sandwich, these mouth-watering pinwheels are filled with corned beef, sauerkraut, Swiss cheese, and tangy Thousand Island dressing before baking until golden brown.

2 packages (8 ounces each) refrigerated crescent rolls
1 package (2.5 ounces) corned beef, chopped
½ cup sauerkraut, drained, squeezed dry and chopped
¼ cup Thousand Island dressing
1 cup (4 ounces) finely shredded Swiss cheese

Preheat oven to 375°F. Unroll crescent dough; separate into 8 rectangles. Press perforations together to seal. Using **Food Chopper**, finely chop corned beef and sauerkraut; set aside. Using **All-Purpose Spreader**, spread about 1½ teaspoons dressing evenly onto each rectangle; top with corned beef, sauerkraut and cheese. Starting at shortest side, roll up each rectangle, jelly-roll fashion; press seams together to seal. Cut each roll into four 1-inch-thick slices; place, cut sides down, on **15" Round Baking Stone**. Bake 20-22 minutes or until golden brown. Serve warm with additional Thousand Island dressing, if desired.

Yield: 32 roll-ups

Approximately 160 calories and 10 grams of fat per serving (2 roll-ups)

Beef and Cheddar Roll-Ups: Substitute smoked beef for corned beef, ⅓ cup green onion slices for ½ cup sauerkraut, 2 tablespoons Dijon mustard for ¼ cup Thousand Island dressing, and cheddar cheese for Swiss cheese.

COOK'S TIP

■ *Crescent roll dough is easiest to work with if kept refrigerated until ready for use. Once the dough is warm, it becomes soft and sometimes sticky, making it difficult to work with.*

A-PIZZA-TEASER

This festive-looking snack becomes a real "hands on" appetizer
when you invite everyone to pull off their own serving.

1 package (12 ounces) refrigerated
   buttermilk flaky biscuits
   Olive oil
1 garlic clove, pressed
½ cup tomato, seeded and chopped
¼ cup green bell pepper, chopped
¼ cup onion, chopped
¼ teaspoon dried oregano leaves
¼ teaspoon dried basil leaves
1 ounce (¼ cup) fresh Parmesan
   cheese, grated

Preheat oven to 400°F. Separate biscuits horizontally in half to form 20 biscuits. On **13" Round Baking Stone**, arrange 6 biscuits, with edges touching, in circle. Arrange remaining biscuits, edges touching, in another circle around center ring of biscuits. Gently press biscuits together with fingers to seal, leaving outside edges scalloped for petal effect. Using **Kitchen Spritzer**, lightly spray biscuits with oil. Using **Garlic Press**, press garlic over biscuits; spread evenly. Using **Food Chopper**, chop tomato, bell pepper and onion; sprinkle evenly over biscuits along with oregano and basil. Bake 15-17 minutes or until edges are golden brown; remove from oven. Using **Deluxe Cheese Grater**, immediately grate cheese over warm biscuits. To serve, pull biscuits apart.

Yield: 20 biscuits

Approximately 130 calories and 6 grams of fat per serving
(2 biscuits)

COOK'S TIPS

■ *Pressing the garlic allows it to release more of its oils, producing a stronger flavor than if the cloves are sliced or left whole.*

■ *While other forms of garlic (i.e. garlic powder, garlic salt or jarred minced garlic) may be more convenient, they don't measure up to the robust flavor of the less expensive, more readily available fresh garlic.*

TOOL TIP

■ *There's no need to peel garlic cloves before adding to the **Garlic Press**. Just pop the clove, skin and all, into the hopper and squeeze. The garlic flesh will be forced through the holes, while the skin stays in the press. For easy clean-up, simply lift the papery skin out of the hopper using the self-storing cleaning tool before pressing the next clove.*

ATHENIAN ARTICHOKE DIP

Feta cheese adds a distinctive flavor to this thick and creamy artichoke dip.
Serve with the stone-baked pita chip recipe below, or with fresh veggies.

1 can (14 ounces) artichoke hearts in water, drained and chopped
4 ounces feta cheese, chopped
¼ cup red or green bell pepper, chopped
1 garlic clove, pressed
1 cup mayonnaise
3 green onions with tops, thinly sliced
¾ teaspoon dried oregano leaves
¼ cup sliced almonds (optional)

Preheat oven to 350°F. Using **Food Chopper**, chop artichoke hearts, cheese and bell pepper; place in **1-Qt. Batter Bowl**. Using **Garlic Press**, press garlic into Batter Bowl. Add mayonnaise, green onions and oregano; mix well. Spoon into **8" Mini-Baker**. Top with almonds, if desired. Bake 25-30 minutes or until golden brown and bubbly. Serve with Baked Pita Chips, if desired.

Yield: 2½ cups (20 servings)

Approximately 110 calories and 11 grams of fat per serving (2 tablespoons dip)

BAKED PITA CHIPS

5 whole wheat pita bread rounds

Preheat oven to 400°F. Using **Pizza Cutter**, cut each pita bread round horizontally in half. Cut each half into 8 triangles. Arrange pita triangles in single layer on flat **Baking Stone**. Bake 8-10 minutes or until lightly browned and crisp.

Yield: 80 pita chips

Approximately 30 calories and 0 grams of fat per serving (4 chips)

HOT PIZZA DIP

Who can resist this bubbly pizza-flavored dip? Serve it right in the
Mini-Baker to keep it warm until the last bite.

1 package (8 ounces) cream cheese, softened
1 teaspoon dried Italian seasoning
1 cup (4 ounces) shredded mozzarella cheese
¾ cup (3 ounces) shredded fresh Parmesan cheese
1 can (8 ounces) pizza sauce
2 tablespoons chopped green bell pepper
2 tablespoons green onion slices

Preheat oven to 350°F. In **1-Qt. Batter Bowl**, combine cream cheese and Italian seasoning; spread onto bottom of **8" Mini-Baker**. In small bowl, combine mozzarella and Parmesan cheeses. Sprinkle half of the mozzarella cheese mixture over cream cheese mixture. Using **Skinny Scraper**, spread pizza sauce over mozzarella cheese mixture; sprinkle with the remaining mozzarella cheese mixture. Top with bell pepper and green onion. Bake 15-18 minutes or until bubbly. Serve with sliced Valtrompia French Bread or fresh vegetable dippers.

Yield: 14 servings

Approximately 110 calories and 9 grams of fat per serving
(¼ cup dip)

VALTROMPIA FRENCH BREAD

1 package (11 ounces) refrigerated French bread dough

Preheat oven to 375°F. Using **Kitchen Spritzer**, lightly spray inside of **Valtrompia Bread Tube** and caps with vegetable oil. Cap bottom of Bread Tube; fill tube with dough. Place cap on top. Bake, upright, 50-60 minutes. Cool 10 minutes. Remove bread from tube onto **Nonstick Cooling Rack**. Cool completely. Cut into slices with **Serrated Bread Knife**.

Yield: 24 slices

Approximately 30 calories and 0 grams of fat per serving
(1 slice)

VEGGIE-STUFFED MUSHROOMS

If you like stuffed mushrooms, you'll love this flavorful vegetable filling.
For best results, pick out the largest mushrooms you can find.

20 large (1½ - 2-inch diameter) mushrooms
   (about 1 pound)
½ cup broccoli, finely chopped
¼ cup carrot, finely chopped
1 tablespoon onion, finely chopped
1 cup seasoned croutons, crushed
   (about ½ cup)
½ cup (2 ounces) shredded cheddar cheese
⅛ teaspoon salt
2 tablespoons butter or margarine, melted

Preheat oven to 400°F. Cut thin slice from stem end of each mushroom; discard. Using **Tomato Corer**, remove stems. Using **Food Chopper**, chop enough stems to equal ¼ cup. Place in **1-Qt. Batter Bowl**. (Reserve remaining stems for another use.) Place mushroom caps, rounded sides down, in **Deep Dish Baker**. Using Food Chopper, chop broccoli, carrot and onion; add to Batter Bowl. Using **Dough and Pizza Roller**, finely crush croutons in sealed plastic bag. Stir into vegetable mixture along with cheese and salt. Add butter; mix well. Using small **Stainless Steel Scoop**, spoon vegetable mixture evenly into mushroom caps. Bake 15-20 minutes or until tops are lightly golden. Serve warm.

Yield: 20 mushrooms

Approximately 80 calories and 5 grams of fat per serving
(2 mushrooms)

COOK'S TIPS

■ *Use the remaining mushroom stems in soups, salads or stir-fries.*

■ *For larger groups, you may want to double the recipe ingredients and bake in the 9" x 13" Baker.*

VEGGIE-STUFFED MUSHROOMS

Pesto Party Squares

PESTO PARTY SQUARES

This make-ahead appetizer is great for entertaining.

1¼ cups round buttery crackers (about 30), crushed

3 tablespoons butter or margarine, melted

2 packages (8 ounces each) cream cheese, softened

1 container (7 ounces) prepared pesto

1 container (8 ounces) sour cream, divided

3 eggs

4 green onions with tops, thinly sliced

1 plum tomato, seeded and chopped

Preheat oven to 325°F. Using **Dough and Pizza Roller**, finely crush crackers in sealed plastic bag. In **1-Qt. Batter Bowl**, combine cracker crumbs and butter; mix well. Press crumb mixture onto bottom of **9" x 13" Baker**. Bake 15 minutes. Using **10" Whisk**, whisk cream cheese and pesto in **Classic 2-Qt. Batter Bowl** until well blended. Add ⅓ cup of the sour cream and eggs; whisk until smooth. Pour mixture over crust. Bake 20-25 minutes or until center is set; remove to **Nonstick Cooling Rack**. Carefully spread remaining sour cream over hot filling using **Skinny Scraper**. Cool; refrigerate at least 3 hours. Just before serving, cut into squares. Sprinkle with green onions and tomato.

Yield: 40 squares

Approximately 100 calories and 9 grams of fat per serving (1 square)

COOK'S TIPS

■ *A real time-saver for busy cooks, prepared pesto can be found in the fresh produce or refrigerated section of most supermarkets. Made from a purée of fresh basil, garlic, olive oil, pine nuts and Parmesan cheese, this garlicky sauce is the perfect complement to the creamy richness of the cream cheese and sour cream in these appetizer squares.*

■ *This recipe can be made up to 24 hours before the big event. Just prepare the recipe as directed, except for topping with the vegetables. Cover and refrigerate overnight. Sprinkle with the green onions and tomato just before serving.*

■ *To soften the cream cheese, place the unwrapped cream cheese in **Classic 2-Qt. Batter Bowl**; microwave on HIGH 30 seconds.*

CHOCOLATE-APRICOT TEA RING P. 30

BRUNCH

Everyone enjoys a lovely,

leisurely brunch. Luscious

fruits and juices, light crisp

salads and fresh brewed coffee

simply add to the pleasure

of these delightful recipes.

Simplicity is key to effortless

preparation, and our quality

Stoneware helps you create

the most incredible meals your

guests have ever experienced.

CHOCOLATE-APRICOT TEA RING

*Fresh brewed coffee is all you need to serve with this impressive, yet easy coffee cake
filled with tart apricots, sliced almonds and sweet chocolate morsels. Drizzle with
a simple powdered sugar glaze to add a crowning touch.*

½ cup dried apricots, chopped
½ cup sliced almonds, divided
½ cup semi-sweet chocolate morsels
2 packages (11 ounces each) refrigerated breadsticks
2 tablespoons apricot preserves
¾ cup powdered sugar
2-3 teaspoons milk

Preheat oven to 350°F. Using **Food Chopper**, chop apricots and almonds. In **1-Qt. Batter Bowl**, combine apricots, ¼ cup of the almonds and chocolate morsels. Unroll breadstick dough into 2 rectangles on **18" x 12" Grooved Cutting Board**; do not separate dough. Using lightly floured **Dough and Pizza Roller**, lightly roll dough to press seams together. Spread each dough rectangle with 1 tablespoon of the preserves; top evenly with chopped apricot mixture. Starting at shortest side of each rectangle, roll up dough, jelly-roll fashion; press seams together to seal. Place rolls, seam sides down, on **13" Round Baking Stone**. Join ends of rolls together to form 1 large ring. Using **Kitchen Cutters** or **5" Self-Sharpening Utility Knife**, cut from outside of ring to within 1 inch of inside of ring, making cuts at perforations in dough. Turn each section on its side so filling shows. Bake 25-30 minutes or until golden brown. Remove to **Nonstick Cooling Rack**; cool slightly. In small bowl, combine powdered sugar and milk; drizzle over warm coffee cake. Sprinkle with the remaining ¼ cup almonds. Serve warm or at room temperature.

Yield: 12 servings

Approximately 300 calories and 10 grams of fat per serving

COOK'S TIP

■ *This coffee cake is best when served the same day it is prepared.*

TOOL TIP

■ *To serve, slice with **Serrated Bread Knife**.*

CRAN-ORANGE CROISSANT PINWHEEL

As lovely to look at as they are to eat, these buttery croissants are filled with a lightly sweetened mixture of cream cheese, chopped fresh cranberries and orange zest.

Croissants

1	package (8 ounces) cream cheese, softened
1/3	cup powdered sugar
1	teaspoon orange zest
2	teaspoons orange juice
1/4	cup fresh or frozen cranberries, coarsely chopped
2	packages (8 ounces each) refrigerated crescent rolls

Glaze

1/2	cup powdered sugar
1	teaspoon orange zest
2-3	teaspoons orange juice

Preheat oven to 375°F. For croissants, combine cream cheese, powdered sugar, orange zest and juice in **1-Qt. Batter Bowl**; mix until well blended. Using **Food Chopper**, chop cranberries; stir into cream cheese mixture. Unroll crescent dough; separate into 16 triangles. Using small **Stainless Steel Scoop**, place rounded scoop of cream cheese mixture on shortest side of each triangle. Starting at shortest side, roll up triangle loosely to opposite point. Arrange rolls, pinwheel fashion and point sides down, on **15" Round Baking Stone** to within 1/2 inch of edge. Bake 15-20 minutes or until golden brown. Cool slightly. For glaze, combine powdered sugar, orange zest and juice in 1-Qt. Batter Bowl; mix until well blended. Drizzle over warm croissants.

Yield: 16 croissants

Approximately 180 calories and 11 grams of fat per serving
(1 croissant)

COOK'S TIPS

- There's no need to thaw frozen cranberries before using them in most recipes.

- Store cranberries in resealable plastic bags in the refrigerator for up to 1 month, or in the freezer for up to 1 year.

CRANBERRY COBBLESTONE BREAD

Fill your kitchen with the sweet smell of fresh baked fruit and cinnamon bread.
It's the scent that draws families together on sleepy weekend mornings.

Bread

- ⅓ cup dried cranberries
- 2 teaspoons orange zest
- ⅓ cup sugar
- 4 teaspoons ground cinnamon
- 2 packages (11 ounces each) refrigerated dinner rolls
- 4 tablespoons butter or margarine, melted

Glaze

- ½ cup powdered sugar
- 2-3 teaspoons milk

Preheat oven to 375°F. For bread, combine cranberries and orange zest in small bowl; mix lightly. In **1-Qt. Batter Bowl**, combine sugar and cinnamon. Unroll dough; separate into 16 rolls. Using **Kitchen Cutters**, cut each roll into quarters. Place half of the dough pieces and half of the butter in **Classic 2-Qt. Batter Bowl**; toss gently. Sprinkle with half of the sugar mixture; toss to coat evenly. Place dough pieces in **Stoneware Loaf Pan** to cover bottom of Pan; sprinkle with half of the cranberry mixture. Repeat layers. Bake 40-45 minutes or until golden brown; cool in Pan 15 minutes. Loosen bread from edges of Pan; remove to **Nonstick Cooling Rack**. For glaze, combine powdered sugar and milk in small bowl; drizzle over warm loaf.

Yield: 1 loaf (12 servings)

Approximately 230 calories and 6 grams of fat per serving

COOK'S TIPS

- To prevent the crust of the bread from becoming too brown, loosely tent the top of the bread with aluminum foil during the last 20 minutes of baking.

- Dried cherries may be substituted for the dried cranberries, if desired.

CRANBERRY COBBLESTONE BREAD

BOUNTIFUL BRUNCH PIZZA

Shredded hash brown patties form the crust of this hearty breakfast pizza.
Topped with your favorite omelet ingredients, it's simply delicious.

Crust
- 1 package (24 ounces) frozen shredded hash brown patties, thawed and broken apart
- 1 egg, beaten
  Salt and ground black pepper to taste

Egg Topping
- 7 eggs
- ½ cup milk
  Salt and ground black pepper to taste (optional)
- 1 cup chopped ham
- ½ cup sliced fresh mushrooms
- ¼ cup green onion slices
- ¼ cup chopped green bell pepper
- 1½ cups (6 ounces) shredded cheddar cheese

Preheat oven to 400°F. Cover **15" Round Baking Stone** with sheet of **Parchment Paper**. For crust, combine potatoes, egg, salt and pepper in **Classic 2-Qt. Batter Bowl**; mix well. Spread potato mixture into 14-inch circle on prepared Stone; pat down with back of spoon. Bake 20 minutes; remove from oven. For egg topping, whisk eggs and milk in **1-Qt. Batter Bowl**. Season with salt and black pepper, if desired. Microwave on HIGH 3 minutes; stir. Microwave an additional 3 minutes; stir. Spread cooked egg mixture evenly over potato crust; top with ham, mushrooms, green onion and bell pepper. Sprinkle with cheese. Return to oven. Bake 10 minutes. To serve, cut into wedges with **Pizza Cutter**.

Yield: 10 servings

Approximately 210 calories and 15 grams of fat per serving

COOK'S TIP

- *For a special breakfast or company brunch without the last minute rush, assemble the recipe ingredients the night before. For example, place the hash brown potatoes in the refrigerator to thaw. Chop the ham and bell pepper with the **Food Chopper**. Slice the mushrooms with the **Egg Slicer Plus**. Place in separate containers. Mix the eggs and the milk in the **Batter Bowl**. Cover all ingredients, refrigerate overnight and sleep tight!*

BOUNTIFUL BRUNCH PIZZA

BANANA-ORANGE MUFFIN BREAD

This moist, fruit-filled breakfast bread tastes heavenly fresh from the oven, but it also freezes beautifully to serve with coffee when those unplanned guests come to call.

Bread
- 2 cups all-purpose flour
- ½ cup sugar
- 2 teaspoons baking powder
- ½ teaspoon baking soda
- ½ teaspoon salt
- 1 cup mashed ripe bananas (about 2 medium)
- 1 egg
- ¼ cup butter or margarine, melted
- 1 teaspoon orange zest
- ⅓ cup orange juice

Streusel
- 2 tablespoons butter or margarine
- 2 tablespoons sugar
- ¼ cup all-purpose flour
- 1 teaspoon orange zest

Preheat oven to 400°F. Using **Kitchen Spritzer**, lightly spray bottom of **Stoneware Loaf Pan** with vegetable oil. For bread, combine flour, sugar, baking powder, baking soda and salt in **Classic 2-Qt. Batter Bowl**. Mash bananas in **1-Qt. Batter Bowl**. Add egg, butter, orange zest and juice; mix well. Add banana mixture to dry ingredients; mix just until dry ingredients are moistened. Pour into prepared Pan. For streusel, combine butter, sugar, flour and orange zest in small bowl; mix with **Pastry Blender** until mixture resembles coarse crumbs. Sprinkle streusel over batter. Bake 40-45 minutes or until **Cake Tester** inserted in center comes out clean.

Yield: 1 loaf (12 servings)

Approximately 200 calories and 7 grams of fat per serving

COOK'S TIPS

- *For best results, cool the bread in the **Loaf Pan** on a **Nonstick Cooling Rack** 10 minutes. Then loosen the sides of the bread from the Pan with a knife and turn the loaf out onto the Cooling Rack to cool completely.*

- *To freeze the baked loaf, wrap the cooled loaf in heavy-duty aluminum foil, or place in a resealable plastic bag, and freeze for up to 3 months. Let stand at room temperature to thaw.*

ROASTED POTATO WEDGES

This potato side dish couldn't be easier.

2 pounds red potatoes (4-5 large potatoes), unpeeled
2 garlic cloves, pressed
¼ cup olive oil
1 teaspoon dried rosemary, crushed
1 teaspoon dried thyme leaves
½ teaspoon salt
¼ teaspoon ground black pepper

Preheat oven to 450°F. Using **Garnisher**, cut potatoes in half lengthwise; cut each half lengthwise into wedges, each about 1 inch wide. Place wedges in **9" x 13" Baker**. Press garlic over potatoes with **Garlic Press**. Add remaining ingredients; toss to coat evenly. Spread potatoes in single layer on bottom of Baker. Bake 40-45 minutes or until golden brown and crisp-tender, stirring after 20 minutes.

Yield: 6 servings

Approximately 220 calories and 9 grams of fat per serving

LUAU PIZZA

Add a fresh green salad for a satisfying light brunch idea.

1 (10-ounce) thin-crust Italian bread shell
2 cups (8 ounces) shredded mozzarella cheese, divided
1 can (8 ounces) pineapple tidbits in juice, drained
4 Canadian bacon slices (about 2 ounces)
1 cup fresh mushrooms, sliced
¼ cup green bell pepper, chopped
1 ounce (¼ cup) fresh Parmesan cheese, grated

Preheat oven to 450°F. Place bread shell on **13" Round Baking Stone**; sprinkle with 1 cup of the mozzarella cheese. Cover evenly with pineapple. Stack Canadian bacon slices; cut stack into eighths. Arrange bacon over pineapple on bread shell. Using **Egg Slicer Plus**, slice mushrooms. Using **Food Chopper**, chop bell pepper. Grate Parmesan cheese with **Deluxe Cheese Grater**. Sprinkle mushrooms and bell pepper evenly over bread shell. Top with the remaining 1 cup mozzarella cheese and Parmesan cheese. Bake 13-17 minutes or until cheese is melted. Cut into wedges with **Pizza Cutter**; serve with **Mini-Serving Spatula**.

Yield: 6 servings

Approximately 360 calories and 12 grams of fat per serving

OVEN-BAKED FRENCH TOAST

OVEN-BAKED FRENCH TOAST

This make-ahead dish can be prepared the night before, then popped in the oven a half hour before breakfast. It bakes up fluffy and golden in our Stoneware Baker. Top with fresh, succulent strawberries before serving.

1	loaf (8 ounces) French bread
6	eggs
1½	cups milk
4	tablespoons granulated sugar, divided
1	teaspoon vanilla
⅛	teaspoon salt
	Ground cinnamon (optional)
	Powdered sugar
1	pound strawberries, stemmed and sliced (about 3 cups)
½	teaspoon lemon zest
1	teaspoon lemon juice

Using **Kitchen Spritzer**, spray **9" x 13" Baker** with vegetable oil. Using **Serrated Bread Knife**, cut bread into 1-inch-thick slices (10-16 slices); arrange closely in single layer in prepared Baker. In **Classic 2-Qt. Batter Bowl**, beat eggs with **10" Whisk**. Whisk in milk, 3 tablespoons of the granulated sugar, vanilla and salt; pour over bread. Cover and refrigerate at least 1 hour or overnight.

Preheat oven to 400°F. Sprinkle bread with cinnamon, if desired. Bake, uncovered, 30 minutes or until golden brown. Remove from oven; sprinkle with powdered sugar using **Flour/Sugar Shaker**. Slice strawberries with **Egg Slicer Plus**; place in Classic 2-Qt. Batter Bowl. Add lemon zest, juice and the remaining 1 tablespoon granulated sugar; mix lightly. Serve over warm French toast.

Yield: 8 servings

Approximately 200 calories and 6 grams of fat per serving
(2 slices French toast and ⅓ cup strawberry topping)

COOK'S TIP

- *French bread loaves come in a variety of sizes. The very long, thin loaves are called "baguettes." If using a baguette for this recipe, it works best to cut the loaf on the diagonal in order to get large enough slices.*

DILLY SEAFOOD QUICHE

You don't have to get up too early in the morning to make this impressive quiche.

½ (15-ounce) package refrigerated pie crusts
  (1 crust)
4 eggs
1 cup half-and-half
½ teaspoon salt
¼ teaspoon dill weed
⅛ teaspoon hot pepper sauce
6 ounces flake- or leg-style imitation
  crabmeat, coarsely chopped (about 1 cup)
1 cup (4 ounces) shredded Monterey Jack
  cheese
1 ounce (¼ cup) fresh Parmesan
  cheese, grated
1 green onion with top, thinly sliced

Preheat oven to 375°F. Place crust in **Stoneware 9" Pie Plate**. Bake 15 minutes; remove from oven. In **1-Qt. Batter Bowl**, whisk eggs, half-and-half, salt, dill weed and hot pepper sauce with **10" Whisk** until well blended. Using **Food Chopper**, chop crabmeat. Using **Deluxe Cheese Grater**, grate Parmesan cheese. Add crabmeat, cheeses and green onion to egg mixture; mix well. Pour into prepared crust. Bake 25-30 minutes or until knife inserted in center comes out clean. Let stand 10 minutes before cutting to serve.

Yield: 8 servings

Approximately 290 calories and 19 grams of fat per serving

DOUBLE CHEESE GRITS

Y'all gonna love this Southern favorite – it's doubly good!

4 cups milk
1 cup quick-cooking grits
½ teaspoon salt
2 cups (8 ounces) shredded cheddar cheese
1 ounce (¼ cup) fresh Parmesan cheese,
  grated
1 small garlic clove, pressed
2 eggs, lightly beaten

Preheat oven to 350°F. In **Generation II 4-Qt. Casserole**, bring milk just to a boil over medium-high heat. Gradually add grits, stirring constantly with **Nylon Whisk**. Stir in salt. Reduce heat to medium-low; cover. Cook 5-7 minutes or until thickened, stirring occasionally. Remove from heat. Add cheddar cheese; stir until melted. Using **Deluxe Cheese Grater**, grate Parmesan cheese; stir into grits. Press garlic into grits using **Garlic Press**. Stir in eggs. Pour mixture into **Mini-Baking Bowl**. Bake 40-45 minutes or until knife inserted in center comes out clean.

Yield: 8 servings

Approximately 280 calories and 14 grams of fat per serving

Dilly Seafood Quiche

FLORENTINE CHICKEN RING

FLORENTINE CHICKEN RING

An extremely popular brunch ring that features a savory filling of cooked chicken, cheddar cheese, chopped spinach, bell pepper and seasonings.

1 can (10 ounces) chunk white chicken, drained and flaked
½ cup red bell pepper, chopped
1 package (10 ounces) frozen chopped spinach, thawed and well drained
1 cup (4 ounces) shredded cheddar cheese
⅓ cup mayonnaise
1 teaspoon lemon zest
½ teaspoon salt
⅛ teaspoon ground nutmeg
2 packages (8 ounces each) refrigerated crescent rolls

Preheat oven to 375°F. In **Classic 2-Qt. Batter Bowl**, flake chicken with **Pastry Blender**. Using **Food Chopper**, chop bell pepper. Add to chicken along with spinach, cheese, mayonnaise, lemon zest, salt and nutmeg; mix well. Unroll crescent dough; separate into 16 triangles. Arrange triangles in circle on **13" Round Baking Stone** with wide ends of triangles overlapping in the center and points toward the outside. (There should be a 5-inch-diameter opening in center of Stone.) Using medium **Stainless Steel Scoop**, scoop chicken mixture evenly onto widest end of each triangle. Bring outside points of triangles up over filling and tuck under wide ends of dough at center of ring. (Filling will not be completely covered.) Bake 20-25 minutes or until golden brown. To serve, cut with **Slice 'N Serve**.

Yield: 8 servings

Approximately 400 calories and 27 grams of fat per serving

COOK'S TIPS

■ *To remove excess moisture from thawed frozen spinach, hold it over the sink and squeeze it with your hands.*

■ *For maximum flavor, use sharp cheddar cheese instead of a mild or medium cheddar.*

FRUIT 'N OAT SCONES

Wake up to the aroma of tender oat scones fresh from the oven. This simple scratch recipe makes you feel like you're doing something special for your family.

1½ cups all-purpose flour
1 cup rolled oats
¼ cup packed brown sugar
2 teaspoons baking powder
¼ teaspoon salt
½ cup cold butter or margarine
½ cup diced mixed dried fruit
½ cup milk
1 tablespoon sugar
⅛ teaspoon ground cinnamon

Preheat oven to 400°F. In **Classic 2-Qt. Batter Bowl**, combine flour, oats, brown sugar, baking powder and salt. Using **Pastry Blender**, cut in butter until mixture resembles coarse crumbs. Stir in dried fruit. Add milk; mix just until dry ingredients are moistened. Turn dough out onto lightly floured surface; knead gently 8-10 times. Using lightly floured **Dough and Pizza Roller**, roll out dough on **13" Round Baking Stone** to 9-inch circle, about ½ inch thick. Using **Pizza Cutter**, cut dough into 12 wedges; separate slightly. In **Flour/Sugar Shaker**, combine sugar and cinnamon; sprinkle over dough. Bake 15-17 minutes or until golden brown. Serve warm.

Yield: 12 scones

Approximately 180 calories and 8 grams of fat per serving (1 scone)

COOK'S TIPS

- Raisins, currants, dried cherries or cranberries may be substituted for the mixed dried fruit.
- For tender, flaky scones and biscuits, the butter should be cold before cutting it into the dry ingredients.

TOOL TIPS

- To achieve flakiness in pastry, a solid fat, such as butter, is cut into the dry ingredients. Here our **Pastry Blende**r makes it easy to equally disperse the fat throughout the dough.
- Rolling out the dough with our **Dough and Pizza Roller** not only produces more attractive scones, but also helps them to bake more evenly on the Baking Stone.

FRUIT 'N OAT SCONES

Savory Pork Roast with Apple Stuffing p. 50

MAIN DISHES

*The secret to our Stoneware
is evident in these exceptional
main-dish recipes. Flavors
and textures are enhanced,
meats and vegetables are more
tender and juicy, and crusts
are crisper and more evenly
browned than ever before.
You'll be proud to serve these
specially selected favorites for
family gatherings and elegant
dinners alike. Best of all,
we've kept them simple because
we know how busy life can be.*

SAVORY PORK ROAST WITH APPLE STUFFING

A delicious apple stuffing is a perfect complement to this moist, tender roast.

2	garlic cloves, pressed
1½	teaspoons dried rosemary, crushed
1	teaspoon rubbed sage
¼	teaspoon ground black pepper
2	medium red apples, chopped (about 2 cups)
½	cup celery, chopped
⅓	cup onion, chopped
6	cups herb-seasoned stuffing mix
1	cup apple juice
¼	cup butter or margarine, melted
1	teaspoon salt
1	boneless rolled pork loin roast (2½ - 3 pounds)

Preheat oven to 350°F. Using **Garlic Press**, press garlic into small bowl. Add rosemary, sage and pepper; mix well. Remove ½ teaspoon of the seasoning mixture for stuffing. Core and slice apples with **Apple Peeler/Corer/Slicer**; cut crosswise into eighths. Place in **Classic 2-Qt. Batter Bowl**. Chop celery and onion with **Food Chopper**. Add to Batter Bowl along with stuffing mix, apple juice, butter and reserved ½ teaspoon seasoning; toss lightly with **Mix 'N Scraper**. Spoon stuffing mixture into **Deep Dish Baker**. Add salt to remaining seasoning mixture; rub evenly over pork roast. Place roast, fat side up, over stuffing; cover with **Stoneware Baking Bowl**. Bake 1½ hours. Carefully remove Baking Bowl with **Oven Mitts**. Bake 15-30 minutes longer or until **Pocket Thermometer** inserted into thickest part of meat registers 155°F for medium or 165°F for well done. Let stand, covered, 10 minutes before carving with **8" Self-Sharpening Carving Knife**.

Yield: 8 servings

Approximately 800 calories and 31 grams of fat per serving

TOOL TIPS

■ Use the **Pocket Thermometer** to check the temperature of the pork roast. The 10-minute standing time allows the internal temperature of the meat to rise to 160°F for medium or 170°F for well done.

■ To crush the rosemary, place in small deep bowl and crush with **Mini-Tart Shaper**, applying pressure while rolling the round end of the shaper over the rosemary.

CACCIATORE POT ROAST

Possibly the easiest, most tender pot roast you've ever tasted.
Top boneless beef chuck with garden fresh vegetables and your
favorite spaghetti sauce, then bake until fork tender.

1   boneless beef chuck pot roast
      (2¼ - 2½ pounds)
1   tablespoon olive oil
2   garlic cloves, pressed
      Freshly ground black pepper
1   medium onion, sliced
1   medium green bell pepper, sliced
8   ounces fresh whole mushrooms
1   jar (28 ounces) spaghetti sauce
1   package (16 ounces) spaghetti, uncooked
      Fresh Parmesan cheese, grated

Preheat oven to 350°F. Trim excess fat from roast; discard. In **Generation II 10" Frying Pan**, heat oil over medium heat. Using **Garlic Press**, press garlic into Pan; cook and stir until tender. Add roast; cook until browned on all sides. Place roast in **Stoneware Baking Bowl**; sprinkle with black pepper. Using **Vario-Slicer**, thickly slice onion and bell pepper; arrange over roast along with mushrooms. Top with spaghetti sauce. Cover with **Deep Dish Baker**. Bake 2-2½ hours or until roast is tender. Meanwhile, cook spaghetti according to package directions; drain. Place spaghetti on serving platter; cover to keep warm. Cut roast into thin slices; place on top of spaghetti. Using **Magic Mop**, skim any fat from top of spaghetti sauce in Baker. Spoon over roast. Using **Deluxe Cheese Grater**, grate Parmesan cheese over sauce.

Yield: 6 servings

Approximately 820 calories and 24 grams of fat per serving

COOK'S TIP

■ *When you use the **Deep Dish Baker** and **Baking Bowl** together, as covered pieces, you're creating a moist heat method of cookery. This keeps the aromatic components of the meat and seasonings inside to penetrate, making meats and poultry more flavorful. It also results in more moist and tender meat whether you're cooking beef or pork roast, a classic stew with vegetables or a family favorite pot roast.*

PHILLY BEEF-STUFFED SANDWICH

A hearty sandwich that everyone will like. It's especially
good as a halftime treat for football fans.

1 cup green bell pepper, chopped
¾ cup onion, chopped
1 tablespoon vegetable oil
2 garlic cloves, pressed
1 teaspoon dried oregano leaves, divided
2 packages (10 ounces each) refrigerated pizza crust
8 ounces thinly sliced deli roast beef
8 ounces thinly sliced American cheese
1 egg white, lightly beaten
1 tablespoon water

Preheat oven to 400°F. Using **Food Chopper**, chop bell pepper and onion. In **Generation II 10" Frying Pan**, heat oil over medium heat until hot. Press garlic into oil using **Garlic Press**. Add bell pepper, onion and ½ teaspoon of the oregano leaves. Cook and stir 3-4 minutes or until vegetables are crisp-tender. Remove Pan from heat. Unroll 1 pizza crust onto lightly floured surface. Using lightly floured **Dough and Pizza Roller**, roll out crust to 12" x 9" rectangle; cover with half of the beef, cheese and vegetable mixture to within ½ inch of edges of dough. Starting at longest side of rectangle, roll up dough, jelly-roll fashion; press seam together to seal. Repeat with remaining crust and filling ingredients. Place rolls, seam sides down, on **15" Round Baking Stone**. Join ends of rolls together to form 1 large ring; press ends together to seal. In small bowl, combine egg white and water; brush onto dough using **Pastry Brush**. Sprinkle with the remaining ½ teaspoon oregano. Bake 20-25 minutes or until golden brown. Let stand 10 minutes before cutting with **Slice 'N Serve**.

Yield: 8 servings

Approximately 340 calories and 14 grams of fat per serving

Stuffed Mushroom-Spinach Pizza

STUFFED MUSHROOM-SPINACH PIZZA

Impress the family with this colorful pinwheel pizza.
The combination of flavors is unforgettable.

4 ounces mushrooms, coarsely chopped (about 1 cup)

1½ ounces (¼ cup plus 2 tablespoons) fresh Parmesan cheese, grated, divided

1 package (10 ounces) frozen chopped spinach, thawed and well drained

½ cup pizza sauce

1-2 garlic cloves, pressed
Salt and ground black pepper to taste

1 package (10 ounces) refrigerated pizza crust

2 cups (8 ounces) shredded mozzarella cheese, divided

2 plum tomatoes, thinly sliced

Preheat oven to 425°F. Coarsely chop mushrooms using **Food Chopper**. Grate Parmesan cheese using **Deluxe Cheese Grater**. In **1-Qt. Batter Bowl**, combine mushrooms, ¼ cup of the Parmesan cheese, spinach and pizza sauce. Press garlic over spinach mixture using **Garlic Press**; mix well. Season with salt and pepper. Unroll pizza dough; roll into 14" x 10" rectangle with lightly floured **Dough and Pizza Roller**. Place in **Deep Dish Baker** with sides of dough extending evenly over sides of baker. Lightly press dough onto bottom and up sides of Baker; sprinkle with 1 cup of the mozzarella cheese. Cover with spinach mixture, the remaining 1 cup mozzarella cheese and tomatoes. Using **Kitchen Cutters**, make 1 cut in dough at each corner of the Baker, up to edge of Baker. Bring sides of dough together at center and twist to secure to top of pizza. Sprinkle with the remaining 2 tablespoons Parmesan cheese. Bake 15-20 minutes or until golden brown.

Yield: 4 servings

Approximately 420 calories and 15 grams of fat per serving

LATTICE-TOPPED CHICKEN BAKE

Pictured on page 2

*Using on-hand ingredients, this homemade pot pie has
never been so easy! It's done in just 20-25 minutes.*

1   package (16 ounces) frozen vegetable
     combination (such as broccoli, carrots
     and cauliflower)
2   cups chopped cooked chicken
1   can (14¾ ounces) chicken gravy
1   cup (4 ounces) shredded cheddar cheese
¼   cup onion, chopped
⅛   teaspoon ground black pepper
1   package (8 ounces) refrigerated
     crescent rolls

Preheat oven to 375°F. In **Generation II 4-Qt.
Casserole**, cook frozen vegetables according to
package directions; drain. Stir in all remaining
ingredients except crescent rolls. Cook and stir over
medium heat until heated through; spoon into
9" Square Baker. On **13" x 9" Cutting Board**, unroll
crescent dough; separate into 2 rectangles. Press
perforations and seams together to seal. Using **Pizza
Cutter**, cut each rectangle lengthwise into four
1-inch-wide strips; place over chicken mixture in lattice
pattern, folding under ends of strips at edges of Baker.
Bake 20-25 minutes or until golden brown.

Yield: 6 servings

Approximately 390 calories and 21 grams of fat per serving

COOK'S TIP

■ *Have leftover turkey after the holidays? Use
it in this easy-to-fix casserole instead of the
cooked chicken. Turkey gravy may be
substituted for the chicken gravy.*

TOOL TIP

■ *Our **Deluxe Cheese Grater** makes grating
cheddar, Parmesan and other firm or semi-firm
cheeses a snap. Grate the cheese ahead of
time, place in a resealable plastic bag and
refrigerate until ready to use.*

CHEESY TUNA NOODLE CASSEROLE

Try a light version of an all-time favorite that's quick, easy and, most of all, delicious.

4 cups (6 ounces) egg noodles, uncooked
½ cup onion, finely chopped
1½ cups frozen peas and carrots, thawed
1 can (10¾ ounces) condensed cheddar cheese soup
1 can (9¼ ounces) water-packed tuna, drained and flaked
1 can (4 ounces) mushroom stems and pieces, drained
½ teaspoon prepared mustard
½ teaspoon salt
⅛ teaspoon ground black pepper
5 round buttery crackers, crushed (about ¼ cup)

Preheat oven to 375°F. In **Generation II 4-Qt. Casserole**, cook noodles according to package directions; drain. Place in Casserole. Chop onion with **Food Chopper**. Add to noodles in Casserole along with all remaining ingredients except crackers; mix well. Spoon into **Mini-Baking Bowl**. Using **Dough and Pizza Roller**, crush crackers in resealable plastic bag; sprinkle over noodle mixture. Bake 40 minutes or until crumb topping is lightly browned and noodle mixture is bubbly and heated through.

Yield: 4 servings

Approximately 420 calories and 11 grams of fat per serving

COOK'S TIPS

■ *To thaw frozen peas and carrots quickly, drain hot water from cooked noodles over frozen peas and carrots in colander.*

■ *Casserole may be made 1 day ahead, except for topping with the cracker crumbs. Cover and refrigerate. Before baking, sprinkle with the cracker crumbs and bake, uncovered, 55-60 minutes or until heated through.*

Southwest Taco Pie

Southwest Taco Pie

An easy-to-make cornmeal crust is the perfect base for this Mexican pot pie.

Crust

¼	cup plus 1 tablespoon cornmeal, divided
¾	cup all-purpose flour
1½	teaspoons baking powder
½	teaspoon salt
⅓	cup milk
1	tablespoon vegetable oil

Filling

1	pound lean ground beef
1	cup chunky salsa
1	cup (4 ounces) shredded Co-Jack cheese
1	cup shredded lettuce
½	cup chopped tomato
¼	cup sliced, pitted ripe olives
	Sour cream (optional)

Preheat oven to 450°F. Using **Kitchen Spritzer**, lightly spray **Stoneware 9" Pie Plate** with vegetable oil. Sprinkle 1 tablespoon of the cornmeal evenly onto bottom and sides of prepared Pie Plate. For crust, combine the remaining ¼ cup cornmeal, flour, baking powder and salt in **1-Qt. Batter Bowl**. Add milk and oil; stir with fork until mixture forms a ball. Transfer to lightly floured surface. Using lightly floured **Dough and Pizza Roller**, roll out crust to 10-inch circle. Place in prepared Pie Plate; shape edge to form rim. For filling, cook and stir ground beef in **Generation II 10" Frying Pan** over medium heat 8-10 minutes or until beef is no longer pink; drain. Stir in salsa. Spoon beef mixture into pie crust; sprinkle with cheese. Bake 12-15 minutes or until crust is golden brown and cheese is melted. Top pie with lettuce, tomato and olives. Garnish with sour cream and additional salsa, if desired.

Yield: 6 servings

Approximately 340 calories and 17 grams of fat per serving

APRICOT-DIJON GLAZED TURKEY WITH HERBED PILAF

Excellent for entertaining or a special Sunday dinner, this turkey breast is glazed with an easy apricot sauce for extra moisture and flavor.

Herbed Pilaf

- 2¾ cups water
- 6 chicken bouillon cubes or 6 teaspoons chicken bouillon granules
- 1½ cups uncooked long-grain white rice
- ½ cup slivered almonds
- ½ cup chopped dried apricots
- 4 green onions with tops, sliced
- ¼ cup snipped fresh parsley
- 1 tablespoon orange zest
- 1 teaspoon dried rosemary, crushed
- 1 teaspoon dried thyme leaves

- 1 boneless turkey breast half (about 2½ pounds)

Apricot-Dijon Sauce

- 1 cup apricot jam or orange marmalade
- 2 tablespoons Dijon mustard

Preheat oven to 350°F. For herbed pilaf, bring water to a boil. Add bouillon; stir until dissolved. Cool slightly. Pour bouillon into **Stoneware Baking Bowl**. Add all remaining pilaf ingredients except turkey; mix well. Remove any excess fat from turkey breast; place on top of rice mixture. Cover with **Deep Dish Baker**. Bake 45 minutes. Remove turkey from oven; carefully remove Baker with **Oven Mitts**. For apricot-Dijon sauce, combine jam and Dijon mustard in **Generation II 1½-Qt. Saucepan**. Remove ¼ cup of the sauce; brush onto turkey with **Pastry Brush**. Set remaining sauce aside. Return turkey to oven; continue baking, uncovered, 25-35 minutes or until **Pocket Thermometer** inserted into thickest part of breast registers 170°F. Remove turkey from oven. Cover; let stand 10 minutes before carving. Meanwhile, heat remaining sauce over medium heat until warm. Carve turkey with **8" Self-Sharpening Carving Knife**. Stir pilaf just before serving; serve with turkey and sauce.

Yield: 6 servings

Approximately 630 calories and 17 grams of fat per serving

COOK'S TIP

■ *After removing the turkey from the oven, cover it and let it stand for 10 minutes. This standing time will allow the internal temperature of the meat to rise to 180°F, the proper doneness temperature for turkey.*

SMOKED TURKEY QUESADILLA STACK

No one will ever know how incredibly quick and easy this entree is to prepare.

1 medium green bell pepper, sliced
   into rings
1 medium onion, sliced into rings
   Vegetable oil
½ teaspoon chili powder
¼ teaspoon ground cumin
3 (10-inch) flour tortillas
6 ounces deli smoked turkey breast,
   thinly sliced
1½ cups (6 ounces) shredded Co-Jack
   cheese, divided
2 tablespoons plus 1 teaspoon snipped fresh
   cilantro or parsley, divided
   Salsa (optional)

Preheat oven to 400°F. Thinly slice bell pepper and onion with **Vario-Slicer**. In **Generation II 10" Frying Pan**, heat 1 tablespoon oil over medium-high heat until hot. Add bell pepper, onion, chili powder and cumin; cook and stir until vegetables are tender. Remove from heat. On **13" Round Baking Stone**, layer 1 tortilla, half of the turkey, ½ cup of the cheese, 1 tablespoon of the cilantro and half of the vegetable mixture; repeat layers. Top with the remaining tortilla. Using **Pastry Brush**, brush top lightly with oil. Bake 12-14 minutes or until cheese is melted and top begins to brown. Sprinkle with the remaining ½ cup cheese and 1 teaspoon cilantro. Continue baking 1-2 minutes or until cheese is melted. Cut into wedges with **Pizza Cutter**; serve with salsa, if desired.

Yield: 6 servings

Approximately 300 calories and 17 grams of fat per serving

COOK'S TIP

■ *Oven-roasted turkey breast may be substituted for the smoked turkey, if desired.*

CHUCK WAGON CASSEROLE

CHUCK WAGON CASSEROLE

We call this the perfect pantry recipe, because it's made with everything you might have on hand. Circle the wagons!

½ cup onion, chopped
½ cup green bell pepper, chopped
1 pound lean ground beef
1 can (15½ ounces) mild chili beans in sauce
¾ cup barbecue sauce
½ teaspoon salt
1 package (8½ ounces) corn muffin mix
1 can (11 ounces) Mexican-style corn, drained

Preheat oven to 400°F. Chop onion and bell pepper with **Food Chopper**. In **Generation II 10" Frying Pan**, cook and stir ground beef, onion and bell pepper over medium heat 8-10 minutes or until beef is no longer pink; drain. Stir in chili beans, barbecue sauce and salt. Bring to a boil. Spoon into **9" Square Baker**. In **1-Qt. Batter Bowl**, prepare corn muffin mix according to package directions; stir in corn. Spoon over meat mixture. Bake 30 minutes or until golden brown.

Yield: 6 servings

Approximately 410 calories and 12 grams of fat per serving

GARDEN-STYLE MEAT LOAF

Our Loaf Pan makes this veggie meat loaf exceptionally juicy.

1 small onion, finely chopped
2 celery stalks, finely chopped
1 large carrot, shredded
2 garlic cloves, pressed
2 pounds lean ground beef
½ cup rolled oats
2 eggs
¾ cup chili sauce, divided
2 teaspoons dried thyme leaves
1 teaspoon salt
¼ teaspoon ground black pepper

Preheat oven to 375°F. Chop onion and celery with **Food Chopper**. Shred carrot with **Grater-Slicer**. Using **Garlic Press**, press garlic into **Classic 2-Qt. Batter Bowl**. Add onion, celery, carrot, ground beef, oats, eggs, ¼ cup of the chili sauce, thyme, salt and pepper; mix lightly but thoroughly. Shape meat mixture into loaf in **Stoneware Loaf Pan**. Bake 1 hour. Spoon the remaining ½ cup chili sauce over meat loaf. Bake an additional 10 minutes or until meat is no longer pink in center of loaf and internal temperature of the meat loaf reaches 160°F. Remove from oven. Let stand 10 minutes before slicing to serve.

Yield: 8 servings

Approximately 270 calories and 12 grams of fat per serving

LEMON GREEK CHICKEN

This hearty one-dish meal tastes like it's straight from the Mediterranean. Pass a loaf of warm, crusty bread, and there will be no end to the compliments you'll receive.

2 teaspoons lemon zest
¼ cup lemon juice
2 tablespoons olive oil
4 large garlic cloves, pressed
2-3 teaspoons dried oregano leaves
¾ teaspoon salt
⅛ teaspoon ground black pepper
2 medium baking potatoes
1 medium red bell pepper, cut into 1-inch pieces
1 medium red onion, cut into wedges
8 ounces fresh whole mushrooms
4 split (bone-in) chicken breast halves (2½ - 3 pounds)

Preheat oven to 400°F. In **1-Qt. Batter Bowl**, combine lemon zest, juice and oil. Using **Garlic Press**, press garlic into Batter Bowl. Add oregano, salt and black pepper; set aside. Using **Garnisher**, cut each potato lengthwise into 8 wedges; place in **9" x 13" Baker**. Add bell pepper, onion, mushrooms and half of the lemon juice mixture; toss to coat. Place chicken on top of vegetables; brush with the remaining lemon juice mixture using **Pastry Brush**. Bake 1 hour or until chicken is no longer pink in center, brushing chicken and vegetables with pan juices after 30 minutes.

Yield: 4 servings

Approximately 550 calories and 23 grams of fat per serving

COOK'S TIPS

■ *Russet or Idaho potatoes are long with slightly rounded ends and a rough brown skin. Their low moisture content makes them an excellent choice for baking.*

■ *It's not necessary to peel the potatoes for many recipes. Simply scrub them well and pat them dry with a paper towel before cutting them into desired shapes. With the skins left on, the potatoes retain more flavor and nutrients.*

LEMON GREEK CHICKEN

CREATE-A-PIZZA

Pictured on page 2

After tasting this homemade pizza baked on our Baking Stone,
you'll never want to order out again.

Crust

1	tablespoon cornmeal
1½	cups all-purpose flour
1	package (¼ ounce) quick-rising dry yeast
1	teaspoon sugar
½	teaspoon salt
½	cup very warm water (125°-130°F)
1	tablespoon vegetable oil

Toppings

½	pound Italian sausage or ground beef
½	cup pizza sauce
1½	cups assorted fresh vegetables, such as mushroom slices, chopped onion or chopped green bell pepper
2	cups (8 ounces) shredded mozzarella cheese
¼	cup (1 ounce) grated Parmesan cheese

Preheat oven to 400°F. Sprinkle **15" Round Baking Stone** with cornmeal; set aside. For crust, combine flour, undissolved yeast, sugar and salt in **1-Qt. Batter Bowl**. Add water and oil; stir until mixture forms a ball. Place dough on lightly floured surface; knead until smooth and elastic, 3-4 minutes. Cover with Batter Bowl; let rest 10 minutes. Meanwhile for toppings, cook sausage in **Generation II 10" Frying Pan** until no longer pink; drain. Place dough in center of prepared Stone; roll into 14-inch circle with lightly floured **Dough and Pizza Roller**. Spread pizza sauce onto crust to within ¼ inch of edge. Top with sausage and vegetable toppings; sprinkle with cheeses. Bake 16-18 minutes or until crust is golden brown.

Yield: 4 servings

Approximately 615 calories and 33 grams of fat per serving

COOK'S TIPS

■ *Substitute ½ cup pepperoni slices for the cooked Italian sausage, if desired.*

■ *To prepare a thicker crust pizza, prepare dough as directed. Roll into 12-inch circle on* **13" Round Baking Stone.** *Top with sauce and desired meat and vegetables. Bake 18-21 minutes or until crust is golden brown.*

TOOL TIP

■ *It is important to use the right temperature of liquids when working with yeast. If the water is too cool, it will not activate the yeast and the bread will not rise properly. If the water is too hot, it may kill the yeast. By using the* **Pocket Thermometer** *to measure the temperature of the liquid, you can help ensure recipe success.*

OVEN-FRIED CATFISH WITH CAJUN-STYLE SAUCE

This Southern favorite features a "do-ahead" sauce and a bread crumb coating that bakes up nice and crisp on our Baking Stone.

Sauce

⅔	cup reduced-fat mayonnaise
⅓	cup plain low-fat yogurt or sour cream
1	green onion with top, chopped
1	small garlic clove, pressed
1	teaspoon chili powder
⅛-¼	teaspoon cayenne pepper

Catfish

2	eggs
¾	cup dry Italian-style bread crumbs
½	teaspoon salt
2	pounds catfish fillets (4-6 fillets)
	Vegetable oil

For sauce, combine mayonnaise, yogurt, green onion, garlic, chili powder and cayenne pepper in **1-Qt. Batter Bowl**; mix well. Cover; refrigerate at least 1 hour or overnight.

Preheat oven to 450°F. For catfish, beat eggs lightly in **Classic 2-Qt. Batter Bowl**. In shallow dish, combine bread crumbs and salt. Dip fillets into egg, then into bread crumb mixture to coat evenly. Place fillets on **13" Round Baking Stone**; spray lightly with vegetable oil using **Kitchen Spritzer**. Bake 10-15 minutes or until fish flakes easily when tested with fork.

Yield: 8 servings

Approximately 250 calories and 13 grams of fat per serving

COOK'S TIPS

- *Orange roughy, perch, halibut or haddock fillets may be substituted for the catfish fillets.*

- *To prevent **Stoneware** from cracking or breaking, it is important to have most of the surface of the Stoneware covered with food. To allow for even baking, arrange fish fillets evenly, in spoke-like fashion, on the **Baking Stone**.*

PRONTO PASTA BAKE

*A quick and easy alternative to basic lasagna, this layered pasta dish will soon become
a family favorite. It features rotini pasta, ready-made spaghetti sauce,
fresh chopped zucchini and two kinds of cheese.*

12 ounces rotini pasta, uncooked
 2 medium zucchini, coarsely chopped
   (about 2 cups)
 2 garlic cloves, pressed
 1 jar (48 ounces) spaghetti sauce
 1 teaspoon dried basil leaves
 2 ounces (½ cup) fresh Parmesan
   cheese, grated
 2 cups (8 ounces) shredded mozzarella
   cheese

Preheat oven to 375°F. Cook pasta according to package directions; drain. Chop zucchini with **Food Chopper**. Using **Garlic Press**, press garlic into **Classic 2-Qt. Batter Bowl**. Add zucchini, spaghetti sauce and basil. Grate Parmesan cheese with **Deluxe Cheese Grater**. In 9" x 13" **Baker**, layer one-third of the spaghetti sauce mixture, half of the pasta, one-third of the spaghetti sauce mixture and half of each of the cheeses. Repeat layers with the remaining pasta, sauce and cheeses; cover with aluminum foil. Bake 45 minutes. Uncover; continue baking 5 minutes. Serve with toasted garlic bread, if desired.

Yield: 8 servings

Approximately 470 calories and 10 grams of fat per serving

COOK'S TIPS

■ *Casserole may be prepared ahead, covered and refrigerated overnight. Bake as directed except increase the covered baking time to 1 hour.*

■ *For a 6-serving recipe, reduce rotini to 8 ounces, zucchini to 1⅓ cups, garlic to 1 clove, spaghetti sauce to 1 28-ounce jar, basil to ¾ teaspoon, grated Parmesan cheese to ¼ cup and mozzarella cheese to 1 cup. Assemble casserole as directed. Place in* **9" Square Baker**. *Bake, covered, 30 minutes. Uncover; continue baking 5 minutes.*

Pronto Pasta Bake

Crispy Parmesan Chicken Strips

CRISPY PARMESAN CHICKEN STRIPS

*A real crowd pleaser among kids, bake these seasoned
chicken pieces on our flat Baking Stone until golden brown and crispy.*

1½ cups seasoned croutons, crushed
1½ ounces (⅓ cup) fresh Parmesan
　　 cheese, grated
1 teaspoon dried parsley
¼ teaspoon garlic salt
2 egg whites
1 tablespoon water
1 pound boneless, skinless chicken breast
　　 halves, cut into 1-inch pieces
　　 (about 3 breast halves)
¼ cup prepared lite ranch dressing

Preheat oven to 450°F. Using **Dough and Pizza Roller**, crush croutons in resealable plastic bag. Grate Parmesan cheese using **Deluxe Cheese Grater**. In **Classic 2-Qt. Batter Bowl**, combine crouton crumbs, cheese, parsley and garlic salt. Using **10" Whisk**, whisk egg whites and water in **1-Qt. Batter Bowl**. Dip chicken pieces into egg mixture, then into crumb mixture to coat evenly. Arrange on **13" Round Baking Stone**. Bake 14-16 minutes or until chicken is no longer pink in center. Serve with dressing.

Yield: 4 servings

Approximately 350 calories and 19 grams of fat per serving
(4 chicken strips and 1 tablespoon dressing)

HARVEST SAUSAGE CASSEROLE

A short preparation time makes this a perfect weekday meal.

½ pound smoked sausage
2 medium Granny Smith apples
¼ cup onion, chopped
1 can (15½ ounces) great Northern beans,
　　 rinsed and drained
⅓ cup ketchup
¼ cup maple-flavored syrup
1 teaspoon prepared mustard
　　 Dash ground cinnamon

Preheat oven to 350°F. Cut sausage into ½-inch-thick slices; cut slices crosswise in half. Core and slice apples using **Apple Peeler/Corer/Slicer**; cut slices crosswise in half. Chop onion using **Food Chopper**. In **Classic 2-Qt. Batter Bowl**, combine sausage, apples, onion and beans. In **1-Qt. Batter Bowl**, whisk ketchup, syrup, mustard and cinnamon with **10" Whisk**. Pour over sausage mixture; toss to coat. Spoon mixture into **8" Mini-Baker** (dish will be very full); cover with **Mini-Baking Bowl**. Bake 40 minutes; stir before serving.

Yield: 4 servings

Approximately 440 calories and 18 grams of fat per serving

FAVORITE OVEN BEEF STEW

The name says it all. Our Stoneware tenderizes the beef stew meat
and provides a hot, filling meal on a chilly winter day. A loaf of
crusty bread makes this dinner complete.

¼ cup all-purpose flour
¼ teaspoon salt
¼ teaspoon ground black pepper
1½ pounds beef stew meat, cut into
    1-inch pieces
1 tablespoon vegetable oil
3 garlic cloves, pressed
¾ teaspoon dried thyme leaves
1 can (13¾ ounces) beef broth
1 can (14½ ounces) stewed or diced
    tomatoes, undrained
1 medium onion, cut into wedges
2 large unpeeled potatoes (about 1 pound)
2 cups carrots, sliced
½ cup thawed frozen peas

Preheat oven to 350°F. In **Classic 2-Qt. Batter Bowl**, combine flour, salt and pepper. Add beef. Cover bowl with lid; shake to coat beef. In **Generation II 12" Family Skillet**, heat oil over medium heat until hot. Press garlic into oil using **Garlic Press**. Add beef to skillet, reserving any remaining flour mixture. Cook until beef is evenly browned, stirring occasionally. Remove beef and garlic to **Stoneware Baking Bowl**; sprinkle with the reserved flour mixture and thyme. Add beef broth, tomatoes and onion. Cover with **Deep Dish Baker**. Bake 1¼ hours. Meanwhile, slice potatoes into ½-inch-thick slices with **Garnisher**; cut slices crosswise in half. Slice carrots with Garnisher. Using **Oven Mitts**, carefully remove Baker from Baking Bowl. Stir potatoes and carrots into stew; cover with Deep Dish Baker. Bake 1 hour or until beef and vegetables are tender. Stir in peas.

Yield: 6 servings

Approximately 410 calories and 19 grams of fat per serving

COOK'S TIP

■ *To quickly thaw frozen peas, place in strainer and rinse under cold running water.*

TOOL TIP

■ *When uncovering **Baking Bowl**, use **Oven Mitts** and lift **Deep Dish Baker** away from you to avoid escape of steam.*

Favorite Oven Beef Stew

TUXEDO BROWNIE SQUARES p. 76

DESSERTS

Rich moist cakes, crisp cookies, flaky pies, and fruit-filled streusels will be the grand finale to any meal occasion when you use our Bakers, Loaf Pans and Baking Stones. Once you discover how much better baking with Stoneware can be, you'll wonder how you ever lived without it. Try these sweet endings to your many marvelous meals.

TUXEDO BROWNIE SQUARES

*Choose your favorite packaged brownie mix and dress it up with
raspberry jam, fresh raspberries and a silky, white chocolate topping.*

1 package (21 ounces) brownie mix
½ cup seedless raspberry jam
2 cups fresh raspberries, or frozen whole
   raspberries without syrup, thawed
   and drained, divided
3 squares (1 ounce each) white chocolate,
   melted and cooled slightly
2 packages (8 ounces each) cream cheese,
   softened
½ cup powdered sugar
¼ cup milk
1 container (8 ounces) frozen whipped
   topping, thawed
   Chocolate curls (optional)

Preheat oven to 350°F. Lightly spray bottom of **9" x 13" Baker** with vegetable oil spray. Prepare and bake brownie mix according to package directions. Cool completely. Spread jam onto brownie. Reserve ½ cup of the raspberries for garnish; arrange the remaining 1½ cups raspberries evenly over jam. In **Covered Micro-Cooker**, microwave chocolate on HIGH 1 minute; stir. Microwave an additional 30 seconds or until chocolate is completely melted when stirred; cool slightly. Meanwhile, combine cream cheese and powdered sugar in **Classic 2-Qt. Batter Bowl**; mix well. Gradually whisk in melted chocolate and milk with **10" Whisk**. Fold in whipped topping; spread carefully over raspberries. Refrigerate 1 hour or until firm. Cut into squares. Garnish with the reserved raspberries and chocolate curls, if desired. Store, covered, in the refrigerator.

Yield: 15 servings

Approximately 440 calories and 26 grams of fat per serving

COOK'S TIP

■ *To soften cream cheese in the microwave, place 1 unwrapped (8-ounce) package cream cheese in **Batter Bowl**. Microwave on HIGH 15 seconds. For each additional package of cream cheese, microwave an additional 15 seconds.*

TOOL TIP

■ *To make chocolate curls, hold the **Vegetable Peeler** against the narrow side of a chocolate square. Using even pressure, push the blade away from you to create curls. Or, using the large barrel of the **Deluxe Cheese Grater**, grate the chocolate square or semi-sweet chocolate morsels over the dessert.*

SNAPPIN' CRANBERRY-PEAR CRISP

Delightful for fall and winter holiday entertaining, this satisfying dessert has a spicy gingersnap topping. Serve with ice cream, if desired.

Fruit Mixture

1 can (16 ounces) whole berry cranberry sauce
2 tablespoons all-purpose flour
5 medium pears (about 2 pounds), peeled and sliced

Topping

1 cup coarsely crushed gingersnap cookies (about 15 cookies)
½ cup all-purpose flour
2 tablespoons brown sugar
¼ cup butter or margarine, melted

Preheat oven to 375°F. For fruit mixture, combine cranberry sauce and flour in **Classic 2-Qt. Batter Bowl**; mix well. Add pear slices; toss to evenly coat. Place fruit mixture in **Deep Dish Baker**; set aside. For topping, combine cookie crumbs, flour, brown sugar and butter in **1-Qt. Batter Bowl**; mix well. Sprinkle crumb mixture evenly over fruit mixture. Bake 30-35 minutes or until pears are tender and topping is golden brown.

Yield: 10 servings

Approximately 200 calories and 5 grams of fat per serving

COOK'S TIPS

- *Pears to be used for cooking should be ripe, yet firm to the touch.*
- *Apples may be substituted for the pears, if desired.*

TOOL TIPS

- *Gingersnaps can be coarsely chopped using the **Food Chopper**, or place cookies in a resealable plastic bag and coarsely crush with the **Dough and Pizza Roller**.*
- *Peel the skin from the pears with the **Vegetable Peeler** or **Quikut Paring Knife** or they will darken and become tough during cooking.*

CITRUS FLAN CAKE

*This layered dessert is positively exquisite and makes a
dramatic presentation when inverted onto a lovely serving plate.*

Glaze and Custard

1	cup sugar
½	cup water
1½	cups milk
8	egg yolks
1	can (14 ounces) sweetened condensed milk (not evaporated milk)
2	teaspoons orange zest
1	teaspoon vanilla

Cake

1	package (16 ounces) pound cake mix
¼	cup milk
¼	cup orange juice
2	eggs

For glaze, combine sugar and water in **Generation II 1½-Qt. Saucepan**. Bring to a full boil over medium-high heat. Reduce heat to medium-low; cook until sugar turns golden brown and caramelizes, 20-25 minutes. *Do not stir*. Quickly pour sugar mixture into **Deep Dish Baker**; tilt Baker to evenly cover bottom of pan with sugar mixture. Set aside. Preheat oven to 375° F. For custard layer, whisk milk, egg yolks, condensed milk, orange zest and vanilla with **10" Whisk** in **Classic 2-Qt. Batter Bowl** until well blended. Pour over sugar mixture in Baker. For cake, combine cake mix, milk, orange juice and eggs in **1-Qt. Batter Bowl**; mix well. Spoon batter evenly over custard mixture. Bake 30-35 minutes or until cake springs back when touched lightly in center. Cool 20 minutes. Loosen edge with knife. Invert dessert onto large heat-resistant serving plate. Serve warm or cool. Cut into wedges using **Slice 'N Serve**. Store leftover dessert, covered, in refrigerator.

Yield: 16 servings

Approximately 320 calories and 12 grams of fat per serving

CITRUS FLAN CAKE

PUMPKIN CREAM CHEESE SQUARES

Marbled with a cream cheese filling, these moist squares are lightly spiced with just the right amount of sweetness. There's no need for frosting… just cut and serve.

Filling

½	(8-ounce) package cream cheese, softened
¼	cup sugar
1	egg

Batter

1	cup canned solid-pack pumpkin
1	cup sugar
1	egg
⅓	cup vegetable oil
1	cup all-purpose flour
1	teaspoon ground cinnamon
1	teaspoon baking powder
½	teaspoon baking soda
½	teaspoon salt
¼	teaspoon ground nutmeg
¼	teaspoon ground ginger
½	cup semi-sweet chocolate morsels (optional)

Preheat oven to 375°F. Using **Kitchen Spritzer**, lightly spray **9" x 13" Baker** with vegetable oil. For filling, whisk cream cheese, sugar and egg with **10" Whisk** in **1-Qt. Batter Bowl** until well blended; set aside. For batter, combine pumpkin, sugar, egg and oil in **Classic 2-Qt. Batter Bowl**; mix well. Stir in flour, cinnamon, baking powder, baking soda, salt, nutmeg and ginger. Pour into prepared Baker. Drizzle cream cheese mixture over batter; cut through batter with knife several times for marbled effect. Sprinkle with chocolate morsels, if desired. Bake 25-30 minutes or until **Cake Tester** inserted in center comes out clean. Cool; cut into squares.

Yield: 18 squares

Approximately 150 calories and 7 grams of fat per serving

COOK'S TIPS

■ *To soften cream cheese in microwave, place cream cheese in **1-Qt. Batter Bowl**. Microwave on HIGH 15 seconds.*

■ *One teaspoon pumpkin pie spice can be substituted for the ground cinnamon, nutmeg and ginger, if desired.*

LEMON STREUSEL BARS

These luscious bars are a sure way to win friends and influence people.

Filling
- 1 can (14 ounces) sweetened condensed milk (not evaporated milk)
- 2 teaspoons lemon zest
- ½ cup lemon juice

Crust and Streusel
- ¾ cup butter or margarine, softened
- 1¼ cups packed brown sugar
- 2 cups all-purpose flour
- 1½ cups rolled oats
- Powdered sugar (optional)

Preheat oven to 350°F. For filling, combine condensed milk, lemon zest and juice in **1-Qt. Batter Bowl**; mix well. Set aside. For crust and streusel, mix butter and brown sugar in **Classic 2-Qt. Batter Bowl** until well blended. Add flour and oats; mix with **Pastry Blender** until mixture resembles coarse crumbs. Reserve 2 cups streusel for topping; set aside. Press remaining streusel onto bottom of **9" Square Baker**. Spread filling evenly over crust; sprinkle with the reserved streusel. Pat streusel gently into filling. Bake 30-35 minutes or until light golden brown. Cool completely before cutting into bars. Sprinkle with powdered sugar just before serving, if desired.

Yield: 16 bars

Approximately 290 calories and 11 grams of fat per serving

PEANUT BUTTER FUDGE PUDDING CAKE

This flavor combination is a winner. Serve warm with ice cream, fudge sauce and a sprinkling of peanuts.

- 1 package (9 ounces) devil's food cake mix
- ⅓ cup peanut butter
- ½ cup packed brown sugar
- 3 tablespoons unsweetened cocoa powder
- 1 cup boiling water
- ⅓ cup peanuts, chopped
- Vanilla ice cream (optional)
- Hot fudge ice cream topping (optional)

Preheat oven to 375°F. In **Classic 2-Qt. Batter Bowl**, prepare cake mix according to package directions. Blend in peanut butter. Pour batter into **Mini-Baking Bowl**. In **1-Qt. Batter Bowl**, combine brown sugar and cocoa powder; stir in boiling water. Carefully pour chocolate mixture over cake batter. Bake 35-40 minutes or until **Cake Tester** inserted in center comes out clean. Cool 30 minutes. Chop peanuts with **Food Chopper**. Serve pudding cake warm with ice cream and fudge topping, if desired. Sprinkle with peanuts.

Yield: 6 servings

Approximately 380 calories and 19 grams of fat per serving

UPSIDE-DOWN CARAMEL APPLE PIE

▪▪▪▪▪▪▪▪▪▪▪▪▪▪▪▪▪▪▪▪

UPSIDE-DOWN CARAMEL APPLE PIE

Serve this candied apple pie upside-down to reveal the rich caramel-pecan topping.

Glaze and Pastry

- ¼ cup packed brown sugar
- 1 tablespoon butter or margarine, melted
- 1 tablespoon corn syrup
- ⅓ cup pecan halves, coarsely chopped
- 1 package (15 ounces) refrigerated pie crusts (2 crusts)

Filling

- ½ cup packed brown sugar
- 3 tablespoons all-purpose flour
- ¾ teaspoon ground cinnamon
  Dash of ground nutmeg
- 4 large Granny Smith apples
- 1 tablespoon lemon juice

Preheat oven to 425°F. For glaze, combine brown sugar, butter and corn syrup in **Stoneware 9" Pie Plate**; spread evenly onto bottom. Chop pecans using **Food Chopper**; sprinkle over sugar mixture. Top with 1 pastry crust; set aside. For filling, combine brown sugar, flour, cinnamon and nutmeg in **1-Qt. Batter Bowl**; mix well. Peel, core and slice apples using **Apple Peeler/Corer/Slicer**; cut slices crosswise in half. Place apple slices in **Classic 2-Qt. Batter Bowl**; sprinkle with lemon juice. Layer half of the apples in pastry-lined Pie Plate; sprinkle with half of the brown sugar mixture. Repeat layers. Place remaining crust over filling. Fold edge of top crust under edge of bottom crust; flute edge. Cut several slits in top crust. Bake 50-60 minutes or until golden brown. Let stand 5 minutes. Loosen edge of pie from Pie Plate; carefully invert pie onto heat-resistant serving plate. Scrape any remaining caramel topping from Pie Plate onto pie. Cool at least 1 hour before serving.

Yield: 8 servings

Approximately 390 calories and 20 grams of fat per serving

COOK'S TIPS

- ▪ *Place a sheet of aluminum foil on the oven rack below the baking rack where the **Pie Plate** is placed to catch any drippings.*

- ▪ *To prevent excess browning of pastry edges, cover edge of pie with 2- to 3-inch-wide strips of aluminum foil during the last 15 minutes of baking time.*

TROPICAL POUND CAKE

Transform a regular pound cake mix into something special with added mashed ripe banana and flaked coconut. Serve topped with fresh kiwifruit, vanilla ice cream and a drizzle of warm apricot preserves.

1 package (16 ounces) pound cake mix
½ cup milk
½ cup mashed ripe banana (about 1 large banana)
2 eggs
½ cup flaked coconut
6 kiwifruit, peeled and sliced
3 cups vanilla ice cream
½ cup apricot or pineapple preserves, or orange marmalade, warmed

Preheat oven to 350°F. Using **Kitchen Spritzer**, lightly spray bottom only of **Stoneware Loaf Pan** with vegetable oil. In **Classic 2-Qt. Batter Bowl**, combine cake mix, milk, banana and eggs; mix well. Stir in coconut. Pour into prepared Loaf Pan. Bake 55-60 minutes or until **Cake Tester** inserted in center comes out clean. Cool in Pan on **Nonstick Cooling Rack** 15 minutes; loosen edges with knife. Remove from Pan; cool completely. Slice kiwifruit using **Egg Slicer Plus**. Cut cake into 12 slices with **Serrated Bread Knife**. For each serving, top cake slice with kiwifruit slices, a scoop of ice cream and preserves.

Yield: 12 servings

Approximately 350 calories and 15 grams of fat per serving

COOK'S TIPS

■ *For added tropical taste, add 1 teaspoon rum extract to cake batter.*

■ *To warm the fruit preserves, place the preserves in **Covered Micro-Cooker**. Microwave on HIGH 15-30 seconds or until warm.*

Tropical Pound Cake

QUICK CHERRY COBBLER

*The combination of tart cherry pie filling and sweet peach slices
in this in-a-minute cobbler makes this dessert irresistible.*

Biscuit Topping

- 1 cup all-purpose baking mix
- 1 tablespoon plus 1 teaspoon sugar, divided
- 3 tablespoons milk
- 2 tablespoons butter or margarine, melted
- 1 teaspoon lemon zest
- 1/8 teaspoon ground cinnamon

Filling

- 1 can (21 ounces) cherry pie filling
- 1 can (8 1/4 ounces) sliced peaches in juices, drained and cut in half
- 2 teaspoons lemon juice
- 1/2 teaspoon ground cinnamon
  Vanilla ice cream (optional)

Preheat oven to 425°F. For biscuit topping, combine baking mix, 1 tablespoon of the sugar, milk, butter and lemon zest in **1-Qt. Batter Bowl**; stir until mixture forms dough. Combine the remaining 1 teaspoon sugar and cinnamon in **Flour/Sugar Shaker**; set aside. For filling, combine pie filling, peaches, lemon juice and cinnamon in **Classic 2-Qt. Batter Bowl**; mix gently. Microwave on HIGH 3-4 minutes or until hot, stirring after 2 minutes. Pour into **8" Mini-Baker**. Using medium **Stainless Steel Scoop**, drop 6 scoops of dough over hot filling; sprinkle with the reserved cinnamon-sugar. Bake 18-20 minutes or until topping is golden brown. Serve topped with ice cream, if desired.

Yield: 6 servings

Approximately 260 calories and 7 grams of fat per serving

COOK'S TIPS

- *Recipe can be doubled and baked in the **Deep Dish Baker**. Microwave fruit mixture on HIGH 7 minutes, stirring after 4 minutes, before pouring into Baker. Bake as recipe directs.*

- *When baking cobblers, crisps and fruit pies, place a sheet of aluminum foil on the oven rack below the baking rack where Baker is placed. The foil will help to keep your oven clean by catching any juicy drips.*

PEACHY PLANTATION PIZZA

PEACHY PLANTATION PIZZA

Purchased refrigerated cookie dough bakes up to a crisp crust on
our Baking Stone for this summer fruit dessert.

Crust

- 1   package (18 ounces) refrigerated sugar cookie dough, softened
- ⅓   cup pecans, chopped

Topping

- 1   package (8 ounces) cream cheese, softened
- 1   tablespoon powdered sugar
- ½   teaspoon vanilla
- ¾   cup peach preserves
- 1   cup fresh strawberries, stemmed and sliced
- 2   kiwifruit, peeled and sliced
- 2   peaches, pitted, peeled and sliced
- 1   teaspoon lemon zest
- 1½ cups thawed frozen whipped topping

Preheat oven to 350°F. For crust, place cookie dough in **Classic 2-Qt. Batter Bowl**. Chop pecans using **Food Chopper**; stir into cookie dough. Shape dough into ball. Place dough in center of **13" Round Baking Stone**; flatten slightly with palm of hand. Using lightly floured **Dough and Pizza Roller**, roll out dough to 12-inch circle, about ¼ inch thick. Bake 18-20 minutes or until light golden brown. Cool 10 minutes. Carefully loosen cookie from Baking Stone with **Serrated Bread Knife**. Cool completely.

For topping, combine cream cheese, powdered sugar and vanilla in **1-Qt. Batter Bowl**; mix well. Spread mixture evenly onto top of cookie; cover with preserves. Using **Egg Slicer Plus**, slice strawberries and kiwifruit; arrange over preserves along with peaches. Sprinkle with lemon zest. Attach **Open Star Tip** to **Easy Accent Decorator**; fill with whipped topping. Pipe topping around edge of pizza. Cut dessert with **Pizza Cutter**; serve with **Mini-Serving Spatula**.

Yield: 16 servings

Approximately 300 calories and 16 grams of fat per serving

COLOSSAL CANDIED COOKIE

Our flat Baking Stone bakes this giant cookie to perfection. Or, for smaller appetites, try our drop cookie variation.

1	cup candy-coated chocolate pieces
1 1/2	cups all-purpose flour
1/2	teaspoon baking soda
1/4	teaspoon salt
1/2	cup butter or margarine, softened
1/3	cup granulated sugar
1/3	cup packed brown sugar
1	egg
1	teaspoon vanilla

Preheat oven to 350°F. Reserve 1/3 cup candies for decorating; coarsely chop remaining candies with **Food Chopper**. Set aside. In **1-Qt. Batter Bowl**, combine flour, baking soda and salt; mix well. In **Classic 2-Qt. Batter Bowl**, beat butter and sugars until creamy. Add egg and vanilla; beat well. Add flour mixture; mix well. Stir in chopped candies. Place dough in center of **13"** or **15" Round Baking Stone**. Using lightly floured **Dough and Pizza Roller**, roll out dough to 11-inch circle. Decorate with reserved candies. Bake 16-18 minutes or until light golden brown. Cool completely. Carefully loosen cookie from Baking Stone with **Serrated Bread Knife**. Cut into wedges to serve.

Yield: 10 servings

Approximately 260 calories and 12 grams of fat per serving

Candied Drop Cookies: Prepare cookie dough as directed. Using small **Stainless Steel Scoop**, drop dough, 2 inches apart, onto Baking Stone. Decorate with reserved candies. Bake 12-14 minutes or until light golden brown. Cool 2-3 minutes on Baking Stone; remove to **Nonstick Cooling Rack**. About 3 dozen cookies. (*Pictured on page 93.*)

COOK'S TIP

■ *Take advantage of colored candy-coated chocolate pieces available at special holidays and tailor your cookie to fit the colors of the season.*

TOOL TIP

■ *For that special occasion, fill the **Easy Accent Decorator** with prepared frosting and decorate cookie as desired.*

COLOSSAL CANDIED COOKIE

CHOCO-PEANUT BUTTER CUP COOKIES

Nothing tastes better with a tall glass of cold milk than these yummy, oversized chocolatey cookies. When baked on our flat Baking Stone, they're tender-crisp on the outside and chewy on the inside.

1¾ cups all-purpose flour
½ teaspoon baking soda
¼ teaspoon salt
½ cup butter or margarine, softened
⅓ cup peanut butter
¾ cup packed brown sugar
1 egg
1 teaspoon vanilla
1 cup semi-sweet chocolate morsels, melted
8 peanut butter cup candies (0.6 ounce each), coarsely chopped

Preheat oven to 350°F. In **1-Qt. Batter Bowl**, combine flour, baking soda and salt; mix well. In **Classic 2-Qt. Batter Bowl**, beat butter, peanut butter and sugar until creamy. Add egg and vanilla; beat well. Stir in melted chocolate; mix until well blended. Add flour mixture; mix well. Using medium **Stainless Steel Scoop**, drop 9 rounded scoops of dough, 2 inches apart, onto **12" x 15" Rectangle Baking Stone**. (Cookies will spread while baking.) Press 7-8 pieces of candy into each scoop of dough, flattening balls slightly. Bake 18-20 minutes or until cookies are almost set and cracked on top. (Centers should still be moist. Do not overbake.) Cool 5 minutes on Stone; transfer to **Nonstick Cooling Rack**. Repeat with remaining dough and candies. Cool completely.

Yield: 1½ dozen cookies

Approximately 230 calories and 13 grams of fat per serving (1 cookie)

COOK'S TIP

■ *To melt chocolate morsels, place the morsels in **Covered Micro-Cooker**. Microwave on HIGH 1 minute or until chocolate is melted and smooth, stirring every 30 seconds.*

COOKIE TIPS

- *Make sure to preheat the oven 10 -15 minutes before baking.*

- *When baking cookies, do not substitute vegetable oil spreads for the butter, margarine or shortening called for in the recipe. The added water and air in these vegetable spread products can cause cookies to be flat and thin with a tough texture.*

- *Cookie dough portioned with the small or medium **Stainless Steel Scoop** will bake more evenly and produce uniformly shaped cookies.*

- *The first batch of cookies baked on a **Baking Stone** may require a slightly longer bake time. After the first batch, the time range indicated in the recipe should yield good results. For crisp cookies, bake to the high end of the range; for chewy cookies, bake to the low end.*

- *For best results, cool cookies for 2-3 minutes before transferring from the Baking Stone to the **Nonstick Cooling Rack**. This will allow the sugars to become firm and prevent broken or "wrinkled" cookies. Proper cooling of the cookies will prevent the cookies from becoming soggy as the result of excess moisture.*

- *If you have only one Baking Stone, portion the cookie dough onto **Parchment Paper**, cut to the diameter of the Baking Stone. As you remove one batch of cookies from the oven, the Parchment circle of unbaked cookies can be quickly placed onto the Baking Stone and into the oven. Saves time and clean-up!*

- *More than one batch of cookies can be baked at the same time. For best results, position the Baking Stones on separate oven racks but not directly above one another. Rotate the Baking Stones halfway through the baking time to ensure evenly baked cookies.*

CANDIED DROP COOKIES P. 90

SUNSHINE LEMON CAKE

*Watch the smiles appear when you bring on the
Sunshine Lemon Cake. This delightfully refreshing cake is
lemony inside and out, and as easy as pie to make.*

Cake

- 1 package (18.25 ounces) white cake mix
- 1 package (3 ounces) lemon-flavored gelatin
- ½ cup boiling water
- ½ cup cold water

Topping

- 1 package (3.4 ounces) instant lemon pudding and pie filling mix
- 1 cup cold milk
- 1 tablespoon lemon juice
- 2 cups thawed frozen whipped topping
- 2 teaspoons lemon zest

Preheat oven to 350°F. Using **Kitchen Spritzer**, lightly spray **9" x 13" Baker** with vegetable oil. For cake, prepare cake mix according to package directions. Pour batter into prepared Baker; spread to cover bottom evenly. Bake according to package directions. Let cool in Baker 30 minutes. Using metal skewer or large fork, poke holes in cake about 1½ inches deep and ½ inch apart. In **1-Qt. Batter Bowl**, dissolve gelatin in boiling water; stir in cold water. Slowly pour gelatin evenly over cake. Refrigerate at least 3 hours.

For topping, combine pudding mix, milk and lemon juice in **Classic 2-Qt. Batter Bowl**; stir with **10" Whisk** until mixture begins to thicken. Gently fold in whipped topping; spread evenly over cake. Refrigerate 30 minutes. Sprinkle with lemon zest.

Yield: 15 servings

Approximately 280 calories and 13 grams of fat per serving

BERRY PATCH BROWNIE PIZZA

Top this brownie crust with sweetened cream cheese and a colorful combination of juicy berries. It's truly a dessert-lover's pizza.

Crust

1	package (21 ounces) brownie mix
⅓	cup whole unblanched almonds, chopped

Topping

1	package (8 ounces) cream cheese, softened
1	tablespoon sugar
½	teaspoon vanilla
2	cups thawed frozen whipped topping
1	pint fresh strawberries, divided
½	cup fresh raspberries
½	cup fresh blueberries
1	tablespoon vanilla chips, grated (optional)

Preheat oven to 375°F. Line **15" Round Baking Stone** with **Parchment Paper**. (Do not bake without Parchment or batter will run off Stone during baking.) For crust, prepare brownie mix in **Classic 2-Qt. Batter Bowl** according to package directions. Chop almonds using **Food Chopper**; stir into batter. Spread batter onto Parchment to within 1 inch of edge. Bake 18-20 minutes or until set. (Do not overbake.) Cool completely.

For topping, combine cream cheese, sugar and vanilla in **1-Qt. Batter Bowl**; mix until well blended. Fold in whipped topping. Using Food Chopper, chop enough strawberries to measure ½ cup; stir into cream cheese mixture. Spread cream cheese mixture evenly onto brownie. Slice remaining strawberries with **Egg Slicer Plus**; arrange over cream cheese mixture. Top with raspberries and blueberries. Using **Deluxe Cheese Grater**, grate vanilla chips over fruit. Cut pizza with **Pizza Cutter**; serve with **Mini-Serving Spatula**.

Yield: 16 servings

Approximately 330 calories and 20 grams of fat per serving

COOK'S TIPS

- *Parchment Paper, which comes in a roll, is very useful for lining any Stoneware piece. It may be used in conventional or microwave ovens without scorching or melting.*

- *When using Parchment Paper, cookies slide off Stones and cakes lift right out of **Bakers**,* making clean-up easy! The Parchment eliminates the need for greasing Stoneware surfaces.

- *To cut Parchment Paper, place the Stoneware piece on the Parchment and draw around it. Cut out the shape and place it on the surface of the Stoneware.*

INDEX

A

A-Pizza-Teaser, 21

Appetizers/Snacks
A-Pizza-Teaser, 21
Athenian Artichoke Dip, 22
Baked Pita Chips, 22
Beef and Cheddar Roll-Ups, 19
Chicken Satay with Peanut
  Dipping Sauce, 13
Fiesta Nachos, 15
Garden Seafood Pizza, 8
Hawaiian Meatballs, 9
Hot Pizza Dip, 23
Mini Soft Pretzels with
  Honey-Mustard Dip, 18
Pesto Party Squares, 27
Pretzel Stick Twists, 18
Reuben Roll-Ups, 19
Tangy Fruit Salsa with
  Cinnamon Chips, 12
Tomato-Basil Squares, 10
Veggie-Stuffed Mushrooms, 24
Western Potato Rounds, 16
Apricot-Dijon Glazed Turkey
  with Herbed Pilaf, 60
Athenian Artichoke Dip, 22

B

Baked Pita Chips, 22
Banana-Orange Muffin Bread, 36
Beef and Cheddar Roll-Ups, 19
Berry Patch Brownie Pizza, 95
Bountiful Brunch Pizza, 34

Breads
Banana-Orange Muffin Bread, 36
Chocolate-Apricot Tea Ring, 30
Cranberry Cobblestone Bread, 32
Cran-Orange Croissant Pinwheel, 31
Fruit 'n Oat Scones, 46
Mini Soft Pretzels with
  Honey-Mustard Dip, 18
Oven-Baked French Toast, 39
Pretzel Stick Twists, 18
Valtrompia French Bread, 23

C

Cacciatore Pot Roast, 51

Cakes
Citrus Flan Cake, 78
Peanut Butter Fudge
  Pudding Cake, 81
Sunshine Lemon Cake, 94
Tropical Pound Cake, 84
Candied Drop Cookies, 90
Cheesy Tuna Noodle Casserole, 57
Chicken Satay with Peanut
  Dipping Sauce, 13
Chocolate-Apricot Tea Ring, 30
Choco-Peanut Butter Cup Cookies, 92
Chuck Wagon Casserole, 63
Citrus Flan Cake, 78
Colossal Candied Cookie, 90
Cookie Tips, 93

Cookies/Bars
Candied Drop Cookies, 90
Choco-Peanut Butter Cup Cookies, 92
Colossal Candied Cookie, 90
Cookie Tips, 93

Lemon Streusel Bars, 81
Pumpkin Cream Cheese Squares, 80
Cranberry Cobblestone Bread, 32
Cran-Orange Croissant Pinwheel, 31
Create-A-Pizza, 66
Crispy Parmesan Chicken Strips, 71

D

Desserts (See also Cakes, Cookies/Bars)
Berry Patch Brownie Pizza, 95
Colossal Candied Cookie, 90
Peachy Plantation Pizza, 89
Pumpkin Cream Cheese Squares, 80
Quick Cherry Cobbler, 87
Snappin' Cranberry-Pear Crisp, 77
Tuxedo Brownie Squares, 76
Upside-Down Caramel Apple Pie, 83
Dilly Seafood Quiche, 42

Dips
Athenian Artichoke Dip, 22
Hot Pizza Dip, 23
Tangy Fruit Salsa with
  Cinnamon Chips, 12
Double Cheese Grits, 42

F

Favorite Oven Beef Stew, 72
Fiesta Nachos, 15
Florentine Chicken Ring, 45
Fresh Vegetable & Ham Strata, 40
Fruit 'n Oat Scones, 46

G

Garden Seafood Pizza, 8
Garden-Style Meat Loaf, 63